Native American Bibliography Series

Advisory Board

No. 1 *Bibliography of the Sioux,* by Jack W. Marken and Herbert T. Hoover. 1980

No. 2 *A Biobibliography of Native American Writers, 1772-1924,* by Daniel F. Littlefield, Jr. and James W. Parins. 1981

No. 3 *Bibliography of the Languages of Native California,* by William Bright. 1982

No. 4 *A Guide to Cherokee Documents in Foreign Archives,* by William L. Anderson and James A. Lewis. 1983

No. 5 *A Biobibliography of Native American Writers, 1772-1924: Supplement,* by Daniel F. Littlefield, Jr., and James W. Parins. 1985

No. 6 *Bibliography of the Osage,* by Terry P. Wilson. 1985

Bibliography of the OSAGE

by
TERRY P. WILSON

*Native American Bibliography
Series, No. 6*

The Scarecrow Press, Inc.
Metuchen, N.J., & London
1985

PENROSE MEMORIAL LIBRARY
WHITMAN COLLEGE
WALLA WALLA, WASHINGTON 99362

Library of Congress Cataloging in Publication Data

Wilson, Terry P., 1941-
    Bibliography of the Osage.

    (Native American bibliography series ; no. 6)
    Includes indexes.
    1. Osage Indians--Bibliography. I. Title.
III. Series.
Z1210.O8W54 1985   016.973'0497   85-2087
[E99.O8]
ISBN 0-8108-1805-1

CONTENTS

iii

Professor Terry Wilson's bibliography of the Osage is published as number 6 in the Native American Bibliography Series. It contains a short historical survey and a list of annotated materials concerning the tribe from earliest times until the early 1980s. The relative obscurity of this tribe because it was out of the mainstream of western expansion is the reason for the general neglect of the Osages' history and culture among scholars. However, the fact that this bibliography contains over seven hundred entries indicates that they have received significant attention, though understandably not as much as major tribal groups.

Never very numerous, the Osage did, however, produce outstanding warriors who were powerful enough during the eighteenth century to control an area that now comprises Missouri, Arkansas, Kansas, and Oklahoma. Allied with the French, they warred successfully against the Spanish in the south, but westward expansion by colonists after the Louisiana Purchase destroyed their power. In 1825 they were forced to settle on a reservation located between the present states of Kansas and Oklahoma.

Following their loss of freedom, they intermarried with whites so that by 1900 approximately 50 percent were half- or mixed-breeds. When their reservation was allotted in 1906, they attempted to settle into a life of farming, which had been somewhat familiar to them from early times, when they combined farming with hunting on the plains. The discovery of oil on their lands then revolutionized their lives, and by the end of World War I, their oil income was so large that they were called the richest group of people in the world. Some of the uneasiness and personal unhappiness that this wealth brought is evident in the novels of John Joseph Mathews,

the most famous Osage writer. Mathews also wrote the standard history of his people, The Osages: Children of the Middle
Waters.

Jack W. Marken
General Editor
South Dakota State University
Brookings, SD

PREFACE

The Osages were never a numerous people and always difficult for social scientists and historians to classify culturally.
Although they were almost continually at war with their Indian neighbors until the midpoint of the nineteenth century,
they never fought against the United States military. For
these reasons the literature, popular and scholarly, dealing
with the tribe is not large.

In this bibliography I have tried to be as comprehen-
sive as possible. Listed are books and articles published
before May 1984 that treat the Osages particularly or in
some significant lesser degree within the context of a related
subject. Theses and dissertations have been included and
newspaper articles excluded, with the exceptions of a few
signed pieces of special importance on aspects of Osage life
and affairs not elsewhere covered, and about a dozen articles
culled from the tribal newspaper, the Osage Nation News.

The items in the bibliography have been arranged al-
phabetically by author. There are annotations describing and
evaluating most of the entries. Fewer than seventy items
are entered more than once in the listings, which are grouped
under three categories. The first of these, entitled "Archaeology, Anthropology, Culture," is the briefest, containing entries descriptive of Osage tribal life before or largely free
of white influence. The second and largest heading, "History Before 1871," lists items about the tribe beginning in
the seventeenth century, when the Osages lived in what later
became the state of Missouri, through their removal to a
reservation existence in Kansas and departure in 1871 from
there to a final home in Oklahoma. The third section, "History After 1871," includes entries pertaining to the Osages in
Oklahoma and their activities across the nation as many scat-
tered into the Anglo-American mainstream.

In an effort to make this bibliography useful to as many readers as possible, I have written an introduction that offers a chronologically organized summary of the major events and developments in the history of the Osages. Those unfamiliar with the tribe and its major figures and happenings can quickly gain enough information to utilize the listings more readily. The introduction can also be used in conjunction with the Author Index and Subject Index to ferret out each reader's desired entries.

For scholars with a need for primary research materials three major sources should be mentioned. The National Archives in Washington, D. C. houses the vast document collections of the Bureau of Indian Affairs and the Department of the Interior. One of the regional branches of the National Archives, the Federal Records Center located in Fort Worth, Texas has the Osage Agency Records transferred from Pawhuska, Oklahoma. This extensive collection includes the correspondence, reports, tribal council minutes, roll books, and other materials concerning the tribe and its reservation and agency from the 1860s to the 1960s. The third significant source for research on the Osages is located in the Newspaper Room of the Oklahoma Historical Society in Oklahoma City, Oklahoma. Microfilm copies and preserved originals of Osage County, Oklahoma newspapers as well as other state newspapers with articles about the tribe are available. Among the most helpful are The Wah-Shah-She News, published by Osages in the 1890s, The Osage County News, The Osage Journal, and The Daily Journal-Capital.

Rarely is a book the product of the author's work alone, and this bibliographical compilation is no exception. Charles Roberts of Sacramento State University led me to several citations that I would otherwise have missed. Robert Black, my colleague in the Native American Studies Program at the University of California, Berkeley, was especially helpful in locating anthropological entries. Finally, Dorothy Thomas, my indefatigable and painstaking typist and proofreader, saved me from many errors and encouraged me with excellent good humor. All omissions and mistakes are my responsibility and I would appreciate having all such brought to my attention.

Terry P. Wilson
University of California,
Berkeley

HISTORICAL INTRODUCTION

Each group of people in the world that shares an identity distinct from all others has a tradition explaining its origin. The Osages believe that a portion of their ancestors came from among the stars and they called them Tzi-Sho, People of the Sky. The Tzi-Sho came to earth in an orderly descent, organized into three divisions who encountered ga-ni-tha, or chaos. With the guidance of Wah'-Kon-Tah, the mystery force of the universe, they found the Hunkah, People of the Earth, with whom they joined to become Ni-U-Ko'n-Ska, the Children of the Middle Waters, a people with an organized life.

The precise geography of this happening cannot be known; however, archaeology and tribal belief indicate that the Osages migrated from east of the Mississippi River in the Ohio Valley to what is now Missouri. They occupied a series of villages located along the Osage River running through the southwestern part of that state when they were first visited by Europeans in 1673. Apparently the Osages and linguistically related tribes, such as the Kansas (Kaw), Quapaw, and Ponca included in the Dhegiha Sioux, lost contact with the eastern Siouan-speaking tribes when they were forced west by invasions of Iroquoian people. Cut off from the Siouan mainstream and exposed to the influences of nearby Caddoan and Algonquian tribes, the Osages adopted a style of living that made their cultural classification by anthropologists and ethnographers difficult.

In their wooded river valleys the Osages subsisted by hunting and horticulture. Twice each year they ventured out of the forest on to the fringes of the plains, following the buffalo herds for several weeks and carrying back enough meat to supplement the gain from their farming and gathering activities. Soon after contact with the French, the Osages were caught up in the fur trade, acquired horses and

firearms as a result, and began aggressively expanding their territorial range. They came to dominate their Indian neighbors to
the south and west in the future states of Oklahoma, Kansas, and
Arkansas. Semipermanent hunting camps were established in
northeastern Oklahoma along the tributaries of the Arkansas
River in the area that would later be the site of the tribe's final
home and reservation. Although never giving up their forest
dwellings, the Osages spent more and more time on the plains,
going as far west as the foothills of the Rocky Mountains and
adopting many elements of plains culture.

Once tied to the French, whom the Indians called I'n-
Shta-Heh, Heavy Eyebrows (because the Osage warriors shaved
their own heads, including eyebrows, except for a roach of hair),
the tribe experienced many other changes. Their European allies
encouraged the formerly haphazard tribal forays against traditional enemies until constant warfare to enhance the fur and
slave trade became normal. By 1700, and throughout the eighteenth century, Indians of other tribes, the French, and later the
Spanish moving north from Louisiana all recognized that the Osages were militarily preeminent in what was to become Missouri,
Arkansas, and eastern Oklahoma and Kansas.

Taking full advantage of their strategic position athwart
the Missouri River, the tribe extracted from the French
and Spanish anxious expressions of good will in the form of
gifts and diplomatic favors. At the same time they lorded
it over other Indians with their European-supplied horses and
guns. Eventually the Osages grew so arrogant that their war
parties broadened their incursions to include French and
Spanish traders and trappers, ultimately causing the Spanish
authorities in New Orleans to decide upon a policy of chas-
tisement. Feeling that the French, whose influence had
waned in the Mississippi Valley by then, had coddled the
Osages, Anathease de Mezieres, commander of the Spanish
fort at Natchitoches, urged an attack in force employing Indians hostile to the tribe. Never fulfilled, the direct military approach was dropped in favor of economic persuasion.
Attempting to coerce the Osages through a trade boycott
proved fruitless as the tribe's warriors seized the highly desired goods from individual traders who tried to bypass them.

Near the end of 1792, Hector Baron de Carondelet,
the Spanish governor of New Orleans, stiffened the resolve
of his administration to carry out the embargo and eventually, months later, actually declared war on the Osages. Subsequent successes by his adversaries in raiding Spanish set-

tlements forced Carondelet to give up a military solution and
accept the proposal of Frenchman Auguste Chouteau, a long-
time trader among the Osages, to build a fort in the tribe's
vicinity in exchange for an exclusive trade monopoly.   Chouteau and his half-brother, Pierre, enhanced their already
considerable influence with the tribe, erecting the fort in
1795 and convincing the warriors to limit their hostilities.

So prosperous was the Chouteau monopoly that other
traders, especially the Spaniard Manuel Lisa, argued for its
dissolution, a move that finally came in 1802.   By this time,
however, the Chouteaus' hold over a portion of the Osages
was so great that the brothers were able to induce nearly
half the tribe to move to a new home south of their old villages at the Three Forks, the place in present Oklahoma
where the Verdigris and Neosho rivers empty into the larger
Arkansas.

The division of the tribe was effected through a direct
interference with the internal politics of the Osages.   The
Chouteaus had subverted the hereditary claimant for the position of ranking chief, Claremore (Clermont), in favor of
Paw-Hiu-Skah (Anglicized as Pawhuska and translated as
White Hair).   When the latter balked at the idea of moving
part of the tribe, the two Frenchmen turned to a lesser clan
chieftain, Cashasegra, to lead the move.   At Three Forks
the usurper was challenged by Claremore whose heredity
and proven ability as a war chief enabled him to exert control over the Arkansas Band and attract warriors from Pawhuska's villages in Missouri.

The split in the tribe rendered the Osages vulnerable
to another group of white men, the Americans.   Just as
Claremore's band was establishing itself at Three Forks,
the United States added to its burgeoning nation the Louisiana
Purchase.   During the coming decades the tribe would un-
successfully attempt to maintain its sovereignty against the
threats, cajolery, and trickery of the Americans who wanted,
ultimately, not merely the Osage trade and alliance, but the
land.

Without the geographical separation of their population,
the Osages would have been hard-pressed to repel the ad-
vances of the United States.   The tribe had never been a
closely knit people in the sense of a modern nation state.
On either side of the river valley five villages were occupied
by the Little Osages and the Great or Grand Osages; the lat-

ter lived in four related settlements called the Big Hills, the
Heart Stays, the Thorny Thickets, and the Upland Forests.
Each town was divided between the Tzi-Sho and Hunkah, whose
representative chiefs shared civil authority over all five villages.   The two hereditary chiefs of the Upland Forest village acted as titular leaders of the Osages, speaking for all
the tribe in relations with the outside world.

The tribal government did not wield absolute control
over individual Osages.   The heads of twenty-four patrilineal
clans exercised some authority in their role of spiritual leaders.   Each clan lived in specific parts of the villages, acted
as separate military units in time of war, and conducted independent raids against enemy tribes.   This diffusion of authority allowed the Osages much individual freedom and provided needed flexibility for tribal society, but it was easily
confounded by the relatively rigid discipline of the United
States.

Eager to make more land available for settlement in
the eastern states and territories, American presidents from
Thomas Jefferson to Andrew Jackson formulated a policy of
removal.   Unfortunately for the Osages, their lands were
among those that Jefferson promised as compensation for territory in the southeastern states ceded by the Five Civilized
Tribes.   The Choctaws, Chickasaws and Cherokees had in-
truded onto Osage land as early as the 1770s, and the Cherokees became bitter enemies, engaging the Osages in sporadic
warfare until 1825.

In 1808 Meriwether Lewis, governor of Louisiana, and
Pierre Chouteau carried to the Osages the unpleasant news
that the tribal leaders must give up most of their territory
to the Cherokees and consolidate their people's villages in a
smaller area.   The Missouri Osages ceded their claims to
what became the southern seven-eighths of the state and half
the future state of Arkansas located north of the Arkansas
River.   Claremore kept his Arkansas Band aloof from these
demeaning proceedings and his people remained intransigent
until 1818, when exhausted by actions against encroaching
white settlers and enemy tribes, they ceded nearly two million acres to the U. S. , a roughly triangular parcel of land
straddling the present boundary between Arkansas and Oklahoma.

Seven years later, in the late summer of 1825, the
federal government revealed the final solution to the problem

of a continued Osage presence in Missouri: removal to a
"permanent reservation" west of the Mississippi River. Reluctantly the hapless tribal leaders acquiesced to this new ar-
rangement hoping that the "neutral lands," a 25- by 50-mile
rectangular area located just east of the proposed reservation,
would keep the increasing numbers of eastern immigrant Indians away from the Osage encampments. Most of the tribe
moved almost immediately to the fairly capacious reserve,
50 by 125 miles, situated with its long southern boundary cor-
responding to the present border separating Kansas and Oklahoma. The Arkansas Band, however, ignored the reserve,
staying at Three Forks until 1840.

Since the reservation's eastern parts were covered by
forest, the Osages made their homes there, venturing on to
the plains to hunt buffalo as they had always done. Uneasily
settling into their new dwellings, the Osages were gradually
subjected to greater and greater interference from the United
States and its citizens. The office of Indian Affairs had appointed Alexander McNair to serve as the Osage agent in
1824, and a bewildering array of agents and subagents arrived and departed during the next twenty-five years. Re-
senting this bureaucratic intrusion, the Osages, nonetheless,
gradually became dependent on these official representatives
of government to deal with U. S. citizens who began settling
with the boundaries of the reserve.

Cavalry units were stationed near the tribe's settlements to prevent the Osages from personally driving off the
intruders whose numbers escalated rapidly after the organization of Kansas Territory in 1854. The agents could do little
to stem the tide of illegal immigration and another group of
white men, missionaries, worked to sway the tribe away from
violent retaliation. Especially active were the Jesuits, already known to the Osages from their Missouri days. One
of these, Father John Schoenmakers, became particularly influential and was largely responsible for keeping the bulk of
the tribe from joining the Confederacy during the Civil War
despite Albert Pike's success in obtaining Osage signatures
on a Confederate treaty of alliance. Most of the Osages
stayed neutral during the war years, although some fought
for the Union and others the South.

Once the distraction of fratricidal conflict was ended
in 1865, the end of Indian Kansas was assured. Groups of
Anglo-Americans made extralegal deals with individual Osages
"buying" land on the reserve while others merely squatted and

and waited for their government to solve the problems of
trespass.   Treaty negotiations were begun several times,
and in 1868 at Drum Creek the Osages were talked into a
cession of their lands engineered by railroad interests.   This
agreement was later repudiated, but soon afterward a lasting
one was made that called for the tribe's removal south to
Indian Territory, later to become the state of Oklahoma.

Fortunately the tribe had a friendly advocate to look
after their interests on this occasion.   As part of President
Ulysses Grant's Peace Policy of the 1860s, the Society of
Friends (Quakers) was given the primary responsibility for
the administration of Indian affairs.   In 1869 Quaker agent
Isaac T. Gibson arrived in Kansas, assessed the inevitability
of removal, and returned east to lobby for the 1870 legislation that sent the Osages away from their "permanent reservation."   He was partially responsible for the complicated details of removal that included the payment to the tribe of over
$7 million in exchange for the Kansas reserve and the pur-
chase from the Cherokees of land for a new reservation.

Between 1871 and 1873 the Osages migrated to their
last tribally owned home.   They purchased over a million
acres bounded on the west by the Arkansas River in present
northeastern Oklahoma.   The line of the "cross timbers,"
where the eastern woodlands give way to the rolling prairies
of the Great Plains, passed through the new reservation, a
circumstance that softened the Osages' unhappiness at having
been uprooted once more.   Of the 3,000 Osages who moved,
most settled along the streams running across the north central part of the reservation, duplicating as far as possible
the five traditional villages of the past.

The tribe was not destined to live alone, unmolested
by the outside world.   Well-meaning Indian agents and missionaries urged acculturation on them: an acceptance of the
white man's farming economy and belief in the Christian deity.
More welcome to them were traders (some of whom like John
Florer, were with the tribe for years in Kansas) and intermarried citizens, white men accepted into tribal membership
on the basis of their marriages to Osage women.   These
latter and their mixed-blood offspring numbered about 250 at
the time of removal and by 1900 composed over 50 percent
of the population of the Osages.   They increasingly acted as
"cultural brokers" for the tribe, serving as a bilingual and
bicultural buffer for the dwindling group of full-bloods and
greatly altering the substance of Osage culture.

When the buffalo herds disappeared from the southern plains in 1875, it seemed that the Osages might be forced into a sullen compliance with the Indian Office's "civilization" program and becoming farmers to sustain themselves.   However, each member of the tribe received quarterly payments, money representing the interest paid by the U. S. Treasury on the funds placed there from the sale of the Kansas reserve.   Although the amounts were not large, the sums were paid in cash, regularly, on the frontier where money was in short supply.   Before long the agency at Pawhuska was filled with all kinds of visitors on payment days intent on exploiting the Osage recipients.

Additional income came from sales of timber from the reservation's eastern half and more was gained from extensive leasing of the west side's rich pasture land whose proximity to Kansas railheads made it attractive to Texas trail drivers.   With money to support their needs, most Osages eschewed the work ethic of their agents and missionaries, preferring to use their payments to maintain a semblance of tribal sovereignty and culture.   In 1881, led by James Bigheart, the Osages wrote and adopted a written constitution patterned after the Cherokee model, itself a close copy of the U. S. Constitution.

The constitutional Osage Nation endured until 1901 when it was abolished by the Secretary of the Interior.   During its twenty years of existence, the Osages struggled with an inexorably changing universe.   More and more Anglo-Americans came to live on the reservation, outnumbering the tribespeople by the turn of the century.   The eastern part of the reserve, wooded and hilly, became a sanctuary for outlaws fleeing law men from organized territories and states.   Elsewhere in the Indian Territory (divided into two parts with its western portion called Oklahoma Territory) other less affluent tribes succumbed to political and economic pressure and agreed to having their reservations allotted in severalty.

Not until 1906 did the Osages consent to an allotment plan.   They submitted to congressional action that distributed the surface lands equally among the 2,229 persons placed on the allotment roll, retaining the subsurface mineral rights as a tribally owned resource.   This unique aspect of the tribe's allotment had its origin in the discovery of oil on the reservation in 1896 and the slow development of petroleum and natural gas fields during the intervening years.

Oklahoma was admitted as a state in 1907, with the former reservation incorporated along almost identical boundaries as Osage County. An Osage business council, created by the 1906 allotment act, was dominated by full-bloods despite their minority position. Factionalization was rife in tribal politics, but the advent of World War I witnessed a united feeling of patriotism that resulted in a heavy Osage enlistment and creditable showing in the war effort.

After the war a surge in the demand for oil and petroleum products led to a boom in the Osage fields. Production companies bid up to $1 million each for lease rights to 160-acre lots at public auction in Pawhuska. This bonus money, when added to the tribe's royalty on oil and gas production, boosted the Osages' payments in the 1920s causing the tribe to be nationally and internationally hailed as "the richest group of people in the world." Often naive in financial matters and profligate from long practice, the Osages spent their wealth freely on luxury cars, extensive vacations, and questionable appurtenances of the white man's world, including liquor and drugs. The notoriety of the oil boom brought further exploitation to Osage County and, in 1926, a sordid series of murders for profit. The convoluted case, described in the nation's newspapers as "the Osage Reign of Terror," required the entry of the Federal Bureau of Investigation before it was resolved. As the final trial sent the conspirators to prison in 1929, the Osages unknowingly faced an economically bleak future.

The market for petroleum products dropped as dramatically as the rest of the nation's economy in the early 1930s with a consequent drastic loss of income for Osage allottees. Before the end of the decade mixed-blood writer and tribal councilman John Joseph Mathews was heading moves to get relief for his beleaguered fellow Osages. Oklahoma tribes were left out of the Indian Reorganization Act and the Osages were excluded from the Oklahoma Indian Welfare Act. Mathews was able to get a WPA grant to build a tribal museum and meeting house in Pawhuska, now a county seat.

World War II saw Osage patriotism unflagging as tribal members of both sexes hurried to enlist. The few who still had large bank accounts from the boom period supported the war effort generously. Clarence Tinker, a mixed-blood Osage, gained the rank of major general in the air corps before he was killed in action at the Battle of Midway.

The postwar era saw another individual from the tribe gain international prominence in quite another arena--ballet. Maria Tallchief, a mixed-blood, became the foremost ballerina in the world during the 1950s and her sister, Marjorie, also achieved great critical acclaim. Members of the tribe had spread to all parts of the nation, becoming involved in a variety of endeavors, with Colorado and southern California having a special attraction. The largest portion of the Osage population still lived in Osage County or in Oklahoma. Many still returned for the annual June dances, the I'N-Lon-Schka, and original allottees or inheritors of allotments came back to vote in tribal council elections.

The 1970s saw a partial return to the oil wealth of fifty years before. With the Arab oil embargo and resulting energy crisis coupled with new methods of recovery from petroleum fields, the Osages' payment checks rose rapidly. The agency office that dispenses the quarterly payments is now equipped with a computer to handle fractional allotment shares and diverse addresses. Through all the vicissitudes of intertribal warfare, international relations with the French, Spanish, English, and Americans, forced removal and acculturation, oil wealth, depression, and renewed prosperity, the Osages continue their tribal existence as a distinct group of people with a shared history and culture.

BIBLIOGRAPHY OF THE OSAGE

I. ARCHAEOLOGY, ANTHROPOLOGY, CULTURE

1. Anderson, Edward F. Peyote, The Divine Cactus. Tucson: University of Arizona Press, 1980.

   An excellent study of peyote, the hallucinogen, which was used as the sacrament for the cult introduced to the Osages in the 1890s. Contains some specific references to the tribe's use of peyote.

1a. Ashley Montagu, M. F. "An Indian Tradition Relating to the Mastadon," American Anthropologist 46 (1944): 568-71.

   A reprint of an account from an 1841 pamphlet describing an Osage ceremony designed to placate monsters.

2. Astrov, Margot, editor. American Indian Prose and Poetry: An Anthology. New York: Capricorn Books. 366 pp.

   Originally published in 1946 as The Winged Serpent. The collection includes six selections from the Osages, all garnered from Bureau of American Ethnology bulletins compiled by Francis La Flesche.

3. Bailey, Garrick Alan. Changes in Osage Social Organization, 1673-1906. University of Oregon Anthropological Papers, No. 5. Eugene, Oregon, 1973. 122 pp.

   One of the most valuable works on the tribe based on field research and government documents.

4.   Bailey, Garrick Alan.   "Changes in Osage Social Organ-
         ization, 1673-1969. "   Ph. D. dissertation, University
         of Oregon, 1970.

         Emphasizes the effects of white contacts on Osage
         custom leading to the disappearance of a carefully
         balanced social system.

5.   Bailey, Garrick Alan.   "Osage Economic and Territorial
         Change, 1673-1839. "   MA thesis, University of Ore-
         gon, 1968.

         Well-researched with an emphasis on change in the
         internal political and cultural life of the Osages re-
         sulting from the altered economic and territorial
         status of the tribe stemming from contact with the
         Spanish, French, and English.

6.   Bailey, Garrick [Alan].   "Social Control on the Plains, "
         in Raymond Wood and Margot Liberty, editors, An-
         thropology on the Great Plains.   Lincoln: University
         of Nebraska Press, 1980, pp. 153-163.

         The Osage system of governance is described in
         some detail and compared to the systems of the
         Comanches and Cheyennes with the conclusion that the
         Osages had a much more sophisticated social arrange-
         ment than the other plains tribes.

7.   Baird, Donald.   "Some Eighteenth Century Gun Barrels
         from Osage Village Sites, " Great Plains Journal 4
         (1965): 49-62.

8.   Barret, Stephen Melville.   Shinkah: The Osage Indian.
         Oklahoma City: Harlow Publishing Company, 1916.

         This brief book for children is a highly romanti-
         cized fictional version of Osage life.

9.   Beaver, R. Pierce.   The Native American Christian
         Community: A Directory of Indian, Aleut, and Eski-
         mo Churches.   Monravia, Cal. : MARC, 1979.   395
         pp.

10. Beider, Robert E. "Scientific Attitudes Toward Indian Mixed-Bloods in Early Nineteenth Century America," Journal of Ethnic Studies 8 (Summer 1980): 17-30.

   Especially relevant to the Osages since so many were of mixed blood in the nineteenth century.

11. Berry, Brewton, and Carl Chapman. "An Oneota Site in Missouri," American Antiquity 7 (January 1942): 290-302.

   Deals with the archaeology of a Little Osage village as well as some Missouri Indian sites.

12. Berry, Brewton; Carl Chapman; and John Mack. "Archaeological Remains of the Osage," American Antiquity 10 (July 1944): 1-11.

   Locates Osage village sites in Missouri based on historical documents and field work; includes pictures of cultural artifacts.

13. Brandon, William, editor. The Magic World: American Indian Songs and Poems. New York: William Morrow & Company, Inc., 1971. 145 pp.

   Includes five Osage selections.

14. Brazelton, Audra Neil. "Family Life of the Osage Indians Previous to 1872." MA thesis, University of Missouri, 1935.

15. Brinton, Daniel Garrison. The American Race: A Linguistic Classification and Ethnographic Description of the Native Tribes of North and South America. New York: N. D. C. Hodges, 1891.

16. Bushnell, David I., Jr. Villages of the Algonquin, Siouan and Caddoan Tribes West of the Mississippi. Bureau of American Ethnology Bulletin No. 77. Washington, D. C., 1922.

17. Callahan, Alice Anne. "The I'N-Lon-Schka (Playground-
     of-the-Eldest-Son), The June Ceremonial Dance of
     the Osages: A Study in American Indian Arts." Ph. D.
     dissertation, Syracuse University, 1977.

          A much broader study than the title implies, this
          excellent dissertation includes a wealth of informa-
          tion on modern Osage ceremony and custom based
          on extensive field study.

18. Campbell, Lyle, and Marianne Mithun, editors. The
     Languages of Native America: Historical and Com-
     parative Assessment. Austin: University of Texas
     Press, 1979. 1,034 pp.

          David S. Rood contributed the chapter on the Siouan
          languages, of which Osage is one.

19. "Carl Woodring, Upcoming Osage Artist," Osage Nation
     News (Pawhuska, Oklahoma), March, 1978.

          Woodring, a North Carolina resident, grew up in
          Osage County, and his depictions of tribal life have
          made him the best known Osage painter.

20. Catlin, George. Letters and Notes on the Manners,
     Customs and Conditions of the North American In-
     dians. 2 vols. Philadelphia, 1857. Reprinted by
     Ross & Haines, Inc. , Minneapolis, Minnesota, 1965.

          In volume two Catlin offers an excellent descrip-
          tion of the Osages with accompanying sketches.

21. Chapman, Carl Haley. "A Preliminary Survey of Mis-
     souri Archaeology, Part I, Historic Indian Tribes,"
     The Missouri Archaeologist 10 (October 1946): 1-56.

          This survey includes much material on the five
          original Osage villages in Missouri.

22. Chapman, Carl H[aley]. "A Preliminary Survey of Mis-
     souri Archaeology," in Osage Indians. New York:

Garland Publishing Inc. , 1974. Garland American
Indian Ethnohistory Series. Volume IV, pp. 11-172.

This study places the Osage tribe geographically
and culturally within the Missouri area and contains
a large number of photographs of material culture
and archaeological maps.

23. Chapman, Carl Haley. Archaeology of Missouri. Columbia: University of Missouri Press, 1975.

Chapman's specific works on the Osages are the
best available for the tribe's prehistory.

24. Chapman, Carl Haley. "Culture Sequence in the Lower
Missouri Valley," in James B. Griffen, editor, Ar-
chaeology of the Eastern United States. Chicago:
University of Chicago Press, 1952, pp. 139-152.

Part of the article is devoted to the Osages specifically. Chapman places the Osage culture in the
Upper Missouri Phase.

25. Chapman, Carl H[aley]. "Digging Up Missouri's Past,"
Missouri Historical Review 61 (April 1967): 348-363.

Reviews work of previous archaeologists including
ones who worked on Osage village sites.

26. Chapman, Carl Haley. "Osage Prehistory," Plains Anthropologist 7 (1962): 99-100.

27. Chapman, Carl H[aley]. "Osage Village Locations and
Hunting Territories to 1808," in Osage Indians. New
York: Garland Publishing Inc. , 1974. Garland American Indian Ethnohistory Series. Volume IV, pp. 173-
250.

Chapman compiled this study as an expert witness
for the U.S. Justice Department to locate Osage village sites and hunting territories, particularly in the
period from 1804 to 1808.

28.   Chapman, Carl H[aley]. "Osage Village Sites and Hunt-
      ing Territory West of the Osage Line, 1808-1825,"
      in Osage Indians. New York: Garland Publishing
      Inc. , 1974. Garland American Indian Ethnohistory
      Series. Volume IV, pp. 251-294.

            Chapman was employed as an expert witness on
            an Osage claims case and this study concentrates
            on whether the tribe actually lived east of the 1808
            treaty line. He concluded they did not.

29.   Chapman, Carl Haley. "The Indomitable Osage in Span-
      ish Illinois (Upper Louisiana) 1763-1804," in John
      Francis McDermott, editor, Spain in the Mississippi
      Valley, 1762-1804. Urbana: University of Illinois
      Press, 1974, pp. 187-312.

            Has a description of Osage village sites, hunting
            activities, political organization, mourning-war cere-
            mony, and method of warfare.

30.   Chapman, Carl Haley. "The Little Osage and Missouri
      Indian Villages Sites, ca. 1717-1777 A. D. " The Mis-
      souri Archaeologist 21 (December 1959): 1-67.

            Authoritative archaeological description of Mis-
            souri's two most prominent tribes.

31.   Chapman, Carl Haley. "The Origin of the Osage Indian
      Tribe: An Ethnographical, Historical and Archaeo-
      logical Study. " Ph. D. dissertation, University of
      Michigan, 1959.

            The best available study of Osage prehistory.
            Much of this dissertation appears elsewhere in pub-
            lished form.

32.   Chapman, Carl H[aley]. The Origin of the Osage Tribe:
      An Ethnographical, Historical, and Archaeological
      Study, in Osage Indians. New York: Garland Pub-
      lishing Inc. , 1974. Garland American Indian Ethno-
      history Series. Volume III, 338 pp.

Based on extensive ethnographic, historical, and
anthropological research including field study done
in 1939-1940, this study is enhanced by an excellent
bibliography and numerous photographs and illustra-
tions.

33. Chapman, Carl Haley, and Eleanor F. Chapman. In-
     dians and Archaeology of Missouri. Columbia: Uni-
     versity of Missouri Press, 1964.

     This survey includes information on the Osage
     tribe.

34. Connelley, William E. "Notes on the Early Indian Oc-
     cupancy of the Great Plains," Transactions of the
     Kansas State Historical Society 14 (1918): 438-470.

     Discusses the Osage and other peripheral plains
     tribes as well as those whose life was spent almost
     entirely on the plains.

35. Curry, Peggy Simson. "Osage Girl," Saturday Evening
     Post 219 (June 28, 1947): 22.

     Fictional story.

35a. De Voe, Carrie. Legends of the Kaw: The Folklore
     of the Indians of the Kansas River Valley. Kansas
     City: Franklin Hudson, 1904.

     Includes ethnographic notes and summaries of
     myths from several tribes, among them the Osage.

36. Dodge, Reverend Nathaniel. "Religious Notions and
     Traditions of the Osage," Missionary Herald 25
     (1829): 123-124.

     Offers a very ethnocentric view of Osage spiritual
     traditions.

37. Dorsey, George A. "The Osage Mourning-War Cere-

mony," American Anthropologist 4 (July, August, September 1902): 404-411.

Deals with the four-day ceremony of the Osages that featured the celebration of dead warriors by acquiring compensatory scalps.

38. Dorsey, George A. "Traditions of the Osage," Field Columbian Museum, Publication No. 88. Chicago, 1904. 60 pp. Reprinted by AMS Press, Chicago, 1978.

A collection of forty tribal stories with a short preface hardly complimentary to the Osages.

39. Dorsey, James Owen. "A Study of Siouan Cults," in Bureau of American Ethnology Eleventh Annual Report, 1889-90. Washington, D. C., 1894. pp. 361-544.

Discusses the variations and terminology of cults existing in several tribes including the Osage.

40. Dorsey, James Owen. "An Account of the War Customs of the Osages," American Naturalist 18 (February 1884): 113-133.

41. Dorsey, James O[wen]. "An Osage Secret Society," Transactions, Anthropological Society of Washington. Volume 3, 1885, pp. 3-4.

This description of a now defunct Osage elders' society was garnered from Dorsey's 1880s field trips to Indian Territory.

42. Dorsey, James Owen. "Osage Traditions," in Bureau of American Ethnology Sixth Annual Report, 1884-85. Washington, D. C., 1888, pp. 373-397.

Written following an 1883 visit to the Osage reservation, this article taken from oral interviews with tribal elders describes a symbolic creation account in the Osage language with an English translation.

43. Dorsey, James Owen. "Osage War Customs," Science 2
    (1883): 368.

44. Dorsey, James Owen. "Migrations of Siouan Tribes,"
    American Naturalist 20 (March 1886): 221-222.

45. Dorsey, James Owen. "Siouan Sociology," in Bureau
    of American Ethnology, Fifteenth Annual Report,
    1893-94. Washington, D.C., 1897, pp. 205-244.

    The portion dealing with the Osages explains the
    three primary divisions of the tribe, the gens, and
    general social arrangements.

45a. Dorsey, James Owen. "The Myths of the Raccoon and
    Crayfish Among the Dakotah Tribes," American Anti-
    quarian and Ortental Journal 6 (1884): 237.

    Unannotated myth text from the Osage and other
    Siouan tribes.

46. Dorsey, James Owen. "The Social Organization of the
    Siouan Tribes," Journal of American Folklore 4
    (1891): 334-336.

47. Douglas, Frederic H. "An Osage Yarn Bag," Material
    Culture 1 (1938) 26-30.

    Finger weaving, originally with hair but now with
    yarn, is one enduring Osage craft.

48. Drinnon, Richard. White Savage: The Case of John
    Dunn Hunter. New York: Schocken Books, 1972.
    282 pp.

    A fascinating study of a white man presumably
    captured by Indians while very young and brought up
    by them, especially the Osages.

49. Fister, R. G., and G. V. Labadie. Goldenbook of the

Osages. Norman: University of Oklahoma Press,
1960.

A record with Osage music.

50. Fowke, Gerard. Antiquities of Central and Southeastern
     Missouri. Bureau of American Ethnology Bulletin
     No. 37. Washington, D. C. , 1910.

     Includes a discussion of the Osage village sites
     in that area.

51. Fowke, Gerard. "Some Notes on the Aboriginal Inhabi-
     tants of Missouri," Missouri Historical Society Col-
     lections 4 (1912): 82-103.

     Partly devoted to the Osages, the article discus-
     ses the archaeological past and early meetings with
     white explorers.

52. Gayler, Lucy Boutwell. "A Case Study in Social Ad-
     justment of One Hundred Osage Families." M. S. W.
     thesis, University of Oklahoma, 1936.

     Some fairly interesting statistics compiled from
     a study of depression-era tribal families.

52a. Geddes, Alice Spencer. "Recorder of the Red Man's
     Music," Sunset 32 (January 1914): 165-167.

     Comments on the work of composer Charles Wake-
     field Cadman, who collected and transcribed Osage
     music.

53. Gellerman, Elliot. "Early Osage Foundations of Eastern
     Missouri." Ph. D. dissertation, Washington Univer-
     sity, 1937.

     Deals with the archaeological past of the Osages.

54. Graham, Jean. Tales of the Osage River Country.
     Clinton, Mo. : n. p. , 1929.

55. Haekel, Josef. "Uber Wesen und Ursprung des Totemis-
     mus," Anthropologische Gesellschaft in Wie Mitteil-
     ungen 69 (1939): 243-254.

56. Haines, Francis. "The Northward Spread of Horses
     Among the Plains Indians." American Anthropologist
     40 (July-September 1938): 429-437.

57. Haines, Francis. "Where Did the Plains Indians Get
     Their Horses?" American Anthropologist 40 (January-
     March 1938): 112-117.

58. Halkett, John. Historical Notes Respecting the Indians
     of North America. Edinburgh: Archibald Constable,
     1825.

         Especially valuable early work that contains much
     ethnographic material on the Osages.

59. Hamilton, T. M., compiler. "Indian Trade Guns,"
     Missouri Archaeologist 22 (1960): 24-28.

60. Harner, Joe. "The Village of the Big Osage," The
     Missouri Archaeologist 5 (February 1939): 19-20.

61. Harvey, Henry. History of the Shawnee Indians. Cin-
     cinnati, Ohio: Ephraim Morgan & Son, 1855.

         Has a lengthy description of an Osage marriage
     in 1850 while the author was an agent among the
     Osages.

62. Hodge, Frederick Webb, editor. Handbook of American
     Indians North of Mexico. Washington, D. C.: Gov-
     ernment Printing Office, 1910.

         Provides a useful compendium of facts about the
     Osages, their ethnohistory, and culture.

63. Howard, James H. "The Mescal Bean Cult of the Cen-

tral and Southern Plains: An Ancestor of the Peyote
Cult?" The American Anthropologist 59 (February
1957): 75-87.

The Osages were among those Indians identified
with the mescal bean cult.

64.   Hunter, Carol. "Osage Mythology: A Literary Perspective." Ph.D. dissertation, University of Denver,
1978.

The author, a mixed-blood Osage, evaluates the
literary merit of the large body of tribal mythology,
much of it collected by Francis La Flesche.

65.   Hunter, Carol. "The Protagonist as a Mixed-Blood in
John Joseph Mathews' Novel: Sundown," American
Indian Quarterly 6 (Fall/Winter 1982): 319-327.

Mathews was a mixed-blood Osage writer and
novelist whose book Sundown was published in 1934.
Chal Windsor, the mixed-blood main character, struggles with the turbulence of the Osage oil boom.

66.   Hyde, George E.   Indians of the Woodlands: From Pre-
historic Times to 1725. Norman: University of Oklahoma Press, 1962. 292 pp.

Includes a great deal of information on the Dhegiha
Siouan tribes, of which the Osages are one.

67.   Indian Claims Commission.   Commission Findings on
the Osage Indians, in Osage Indians. New York:
Garland Publishing Inc., 1974. Garland American
Indian Ethnohistory Series. Volume V, 494 pp.

These findings are primarily concerned with de-
termining the village sites and hunting territories of
the Osages during the period before 1825, for the
purpose of awarding a tribal claim of compensation
for lost lands.

68.   "Indians Retain Strange Rites," The American Indian
      (Tulsa, Oklahoma) 2 (1928): 13.

          This article deals briefly with the Osage funeral
      ceremony that included painting the face of the de-
      ceased and wrapping the body in a blanket before
      burial.

69.   Ingenthron, Elmo. Indians of the Ozark Plateau. Point
      Lookout, Mo.: School of the Oxarks Press, 1970.
      182 pp.

          Primarily archaeological and historical, there is
      a good chapter on Osage ceremonialism.

70.   Irving, Washington. A Tour on the Prairies. Norman:
      University of Oklahoma Press, 1956. 214 pp.

          Irving visited the Osages and devotes a lengthy
      part of his work to describing their villages, per-
      sonal appearance, and customs.

71.   Judson, Katharine Berry. Myths and Legends of the
      Great Plains. Chicago: A. C. McClurg & Co.,
      1913. 205 pp.

          Includes the Osage creation account and the story
      of the origin of the two main divisions of the tribe.

72.   Klein, Bernard, and Daniel Icolari, editors. Reference
      Encyclopedia of the American Indian. New York:
      B. Klein and Company, 1967. 536 pp.

          Arranged topically, there are several references
      to the Osages.

73.   Kroeber, Alfred L. Cultural and Natural Areas of Na-
      tive North America. Berkeley: University of Cali-
      fornia Press, 1939. 242 pp.

          Volume 38 of the University of California Publica-
      tions Series, Kroeber's overview includes the Osages,

noting how difficult it is to classify the tribe according to culture and geography.

74. La Barre, Weston. The Peyote Cult. Fourth edition enlarged. New York: Archon Books, 1975. 296 pp.

There are numerous specific references to the Osage peyotists in this volume, which combines the author's original work with a reprinting of later articles.

75. La Farge, Oliver. A Pictorial History of the American Indians. New York: Crown Publishers, 1956. 272 pp.

76. La Flesche, Francis. "A Dictionary of the Osage Language," Bureau of American Ethnology Bulletin 109, Washington, D. C. , 1932. 406 pp.

Reprinted in the Indian Tribal Series, Phoenix Arizona, 1975. This valuable work includes Osage-English and English-Osage dictionaries, a phonetic key, a listing of sayings and experiences, and a few tribal stories and legends.

77. La Flesche, Francis. Ethnology of the Osage Indian. Smithsonian Institution. Miscellaneous Collections 76. Washington, D. C. , 1924.

The author's work, stemming from field observations, is the primary source for historians and anthropologists interested in the Osages.

78. La Flesche, Francis. "Omaha and Osage Traditions of Separation," Proceedings of the Nineteenth International Congress of Americanists. Washington, D. C. , 1917, pp. 459-462.

The author did exhaustive research among both related Siouan tribes, studying their points of cultural similarity and dissimilarity.

79. La Flesche, Francis. "Osage Marriage Customs,"
     American Anthropologist 14 (1912): 127-130.

         Tribal women have a very distinctive dress for
     weddings and the traditional ceremonies were quite
     elaborate. Early marriages arranged for girls were
     still common when this article was written; polygamy
     had virtually died out.

80. La Flesche, Francis. "Researches Among the Osage,"
     In Smithsonian Miscellaneous Collections. Volume
     70, No. 2. Washington, D. C. , 1918, pp. 110-113,
     118-119.

         Brief notes on the author's extensive work record-
     ing and translating Osage ceremonial songs and chants.

81. La Flesche, Francis. "Right and Left in Osage Cere-
     monies," in Holmes Anniversary Volume. Washing-
     ton, D. C. , 1916, pp. 278-288.

         The author spent years studying the Osage cere-
     monies and translating them into English.

82. La Flesche, Francis. "Right and Left in Osage Cere-
     monies," in Rodney Needham, editor. Right and
     Left. Chicago: University of Chicago Press, 1973,
     pp. 32-42.

         Taken from La Flesche's ethnographic work from
     the early twentieth century.

83. La Flesche, Francis. "The Osage Tribe: Rite of the
     Chiefs; Sayings of the Ancient Men," Bureau of Amer-
     ican Ethnology, Thirty-Sixth Annual Report, 1914-
     1915. Washington, D. C. , 1921, pp. 35-604.

         Offers an allegorical story of the Osage form of
     governance in the Osage language, in free transla-
     tion, and in literal translation. This is the best
     available source for information on the internal struc-
     ture of the tribe.

84. La Flesche, Francis. "The Osage Tribe: Rite of Vigil,"
     in Bureau of American Ethnology Thirty-ninth Annual
     Report. Washington, D. C. , 1925, pp. 31-636.

         Included are a brief introduction by La Flesche,
         a free English translation of the rite of vigil, the
         rite in Osage taken from dictaphone records, and a
         literal translation into English. Several good photo-
         graphs enhance this work.

85. La Flesche, Francis. "The Osage Tribe: Rite of the
     Wa-Xo'-Be," in Bureau of American Ethnology Forty-
     fifth Annual Report, 1927-1928. Washington, D. C. ,
     1930, pp. 523-833.

         Illustrated with excellent photographs of Osages
         and tribal ornaments and implements, this rite is
         offered in English and Osage.

86. La Flesche, Francis. "The Osage Tribe: Two Versions
     of the Child Naming Rite," in Bureau of American
     Ethnology Forty-third Annual Report. Washington,
     D. C. , 1928, pp. 23-164.

         These important Osage ceremonies were recorded
         from two full-bloods, neither of whom was an English-
         speaker, offering the words in English and Osage.
         Some good photographs.

87. La Flesche, Francis. "The Symbolic Man of the Osage
     Tribe," Art and Archaeology 9 (February 1920): 68-
     72.

88. La Flesche, Francis. "Tribal Rites of the Osage In-
     dians," Smithsonian Miscellaneous Collections 48
     (1918): 84-90.

         An unfortunately brief discussion of the author's
         extensive research effort that resulted in hundreds
         of pages of Osage ceremony being recorded and trans-
         lated.

89. La Flesche, Francis. "War Ceremony and Peace Cer-

emony of the Osage Indians," Bureau of American
Ethnology Bulletin 101.   2 vols.   Washington, D.C.,
1939, pp. 3-255; pp. 3-280.

The best source for information about Osage cere-
monial life with explanations of the various ceremonies, the songs with music scores and translations,
and numerous pictures.

90.   Leitch, Barbara.   A Concise Dictionary of Indian Tribes
of North America.   Algonac, Mich.:   Reference Publications, Inc., 1979.   646 pp.

Arranged by tribe, the entry for the Osages is
three pages.

91.   Levitas, Gloria; Frank R. Vivelo; and Jacqueline J.
Vivelo, editors.   American Indian Prose and Poetry:
We Wait in Darkness.   New York: G. P. Putnam's
Sons, 1974.   325 pp.

Contains a few stories and poems from the Osages.

91a.   "The Lord's Prayer in Osage," The American Indian
(Tulsa, Oklahoma) 3 (1929):   4.

92.   Lowie, Robert H.   Indians of the Plains.   Garden City,
N.Y.:   The Natural History Press, 1954.   258 pp.

Originally published as an anthropological handbook
by the American Museum of Natural History, this
work offers a basic introduction to the culture of the
plains tribes including the Osages.

92a.   Marriott, Alice.   "Dancing Makes Fun," in Franz Boas
and Donald Day, editors, From Hell to Breakfast.
Publications of the Texas Folklore Society, No. 19
(1944):   82-87.

Describes an Osage dance in honor of Mother's
Day.

93. Marriott, Alice. Osage Research Report and Bibliog-
     raphy of Basic Research References, in Osage In-
     dians. New York: Garland Publishing Inc. , 1974.
     Garland American Indian Ethnohistory Series. Volume
     II, 270 pp.

         Primarily an anthropological study, it is directed
         toward defining the geographical area inhabited by
         the Osages and incorporates primary research, in-
         cluding oral sources. The bibliography lists over
         250 items.

94. Marriott, Alice, and Carol K. Rachlin. Plains Indian
     Mythology. New York: Thomas Y. Crowell Company,
     1975. 194 pp.

         Two of the selections are from the Osages, a
         creation account and a story involving a female cap-
         tive who rose to prominence in the tribe.

95. Mathews, John Joseph. The Osages: Children of the
     Middle Waters. Norman: University of Oklahoma
     Press, 1961. 823 pp. Paperback edition by Univer-
     sity of Oklahoma Press, 1981.

         Written by a mixed-blood Osage, it contains a
         massive amount of ethnohistorical and cultural infor-
         mation spanning the period before white contact to
         1920, presented in an almost ahistorical literary style.
         It contains invaluable insights gained from the au-
         thor's numerous interviews with members of his tribe.

96. McGee, W. S. "Siouan Indians: A Preliminary Sketch"
     in the Bureau of American Ethnology Fifteenth Annual
     Report. Washington, D. C. , 1897, pp. 153-204.

         The Osages, a Dhegiha Sioux tribe, are included
         in this discussion.

97. Mead, Margaret, and Ruth Bunzel, editors. The Golden
     Age of American Anthropology. New York: George
     Braziller, 1960. 630 pp.

Includes a portion of the Osage "Rite of the Chiefs" recorded by Francis La Flesche.

98. Montgomery, William B. , and William C. Requa. Wash-ashe Wagerassa Pahugreh Tee (The Osage First Book). Boston: Crocker & Brewster, 1834. 126 pp.

This was printed for the American Board of Commissioners for Foreign Missions and is basically a transliteration of Osage-English sentences and biblical passages in Osage.

99. Morrison, T. F. "Osage Tribal Rites, Oklahoma: Explorations and Field Work of the Smithsonian Institution in 1919," Smithsonian Miscellaneous Collections 72 (1920): 72-73.

100. Moses, L. G. "Jack Wilson and the Indian Service: The Response of the BIA to the Ghost Dance Prophet," American Indian Quarterly 5 (November 1979): 295-316.

Wilson introduced the peyote cult to the Osages.

101. "Most Elaborate Indian Costume in Oklahoma," The American Indian (February 1927): 4.

Has a brief description and a picture of Osage Pahsetopah's costume valued at $2,500.

102. Murdoch, George Peter, and Timothy J. O'Leary. Ethnographic Bibliography of North America. 5 vols. New Haven, Conn.: Human Relations Area Files Press, 1975. 455 pp.

103. Myer, W. E. "Archaeological Field Work in South Dakota and Missouri: Exploration and Field Work of the Smithsonian Institution in 1921," Smithsonian Miscellaneous Collections 72 (1922): 117-125.

104.   Nett, Betty R. "Historical Changes in the Osage Kin-
       ship System," Southwestern Journal of Anthropology
       8 (1952): 164-181.

       From field work in Osage County, this study em-
       phasizes how the tribe's kinship system was altered
       by the economic changes wrought by oil money.

105.   Nett, Betty R. "Osage Kinship." MA thesis, Uni-
       versity of Oklahoma, 1951.

       Based on field work done in Osage County, this
       study combines history, ethnohistory, and linguistics
       to trace changes in the tribe's kinship patterns.

106.   Newcomb, William W. , Jr. North American Indians:
       An Anthropological Perspective. Pacific Palisades,
       Cal. : Goodyear Publishing Company, 1974. 278
       pp.

107.   "Osage Indian Legend," Bulletin of the Missouri His-
       torical Society 4 (January 1948): 92.

       A reprinting from Isaac McCoy's 1840 book on
       Baptist missions. The legend was told by Belle
       Ouiseau, an Osage chief.

108.   "Osage Planting Song," Indians at Work 2 (1935): 34.

109.   Pilling, James Constantine. Bibliography of the Siouan
       Languages. Washington, D. C. : Government Print-
       ing Office, 1887. 25 pp.

109a. Pinkley-Call, Cora. "Stories About the Origin of
       Eureka Springs," Arkansas Historical Quarterly 5
       (1946): 297-307.

       Contains an account of an Osage myth.

110.   Ponziglione, Paul N. "Osage Indian Manners and Cus-

toms," St. Louis Catholic Historical Review 4 (1922): 130-141.

Based on the records of Felix Ponziglione and other Jesuits at the Osage Mission in Kansas during the 1850s and 1860s, this is a valuable piece of descriptive information.

111. Revard, Carter. "History, Myth, and Identity Among Osages and Other Peoples," Denver Quarterly 4 (Winter 1980): 84-97.

This is a thoughtful analysis of self-identification among Indian people as compared to non-Indians. Revard, a mixed-blood Osage, uses the naming ceremony of his tribe to explain how children were instructed about Osage history and their place in the world of the tribe.

112. Rohrer, J. H. "The Test Intelligence of Osage Indians," Journal of Social Psychology 16 (Spring 1959): 99-105.

113. Rothenberg, Jerome, editor. Shaking the Pumpkin: Traditional Poetry of the Indian North Americas. New York: Doubleday & Company, Inc., 1972. 475 pp.

The sole Osage selection is a portion of the "Ceremony of Sending: A Simultaneity for Twenty Choruses."

114. Rydjord, John. Indian Place-Names. Norman: University of Oklahoma Press, 1968. 380 pp.

There is an entire chapter devoted to the Osages and their chiefs relating to linguistics and word origins.

115. Sanders, Thomas E., and Walter W. Peek, editors. Literature of the American Indian. New York: Glencoe Press, 1973. 534 pp.

Included in this collection is the Osage creation account.

116. Sebbelov, Gerda. "The Osage War Dance," The Museum Journal of the University of Pennsylvania 2 (September 1911): 71-74.

117. Slotkin, J. S. The Peyote Religion. Glencoe, Ill.: The Free Press, 1956.

The Osages became peyotists in the early 1890s and the cult has persisted, although diminished in numbers, to the present.

117a. Smith, Maurice Greer. "Political Organization of the Plains Indians, with Special Reference to the Council," University of Nebraska Studies. 24 (January-April 1924): 3-84.

Includes mythic and ritual aspects of political structure with special emphasis on the Osage.

118. Snyder, J. F. "Were the Osage Mound Builders?" in Annual Report of the Board of Regents of the Smithsonian Institution, 1888. Washington, D.C., 1889, pp. 587-596.

119. "Specimen of the Poetry and Singing of the Osages," Archaeologica Americana. Transactions and Collections, American Antiquarian Society, Volume I. Chicago, 1820, pp. 311-317.

120. Speck, T. G. "Notes on the Ethnology of the Osage Indians," in Transactions of the Free Museum of Science and Art of the University of Pennsylvania. Volume II. Philadelphia, 1907.

121. Spencer, Joab. "Missouri's Aboriginal Inhabitants," Missouri Historical Review 3 (1908-1909): 275-292; 4 (1909-1910): 18-28.

Includes a good deal on the Osages of an ethnographic and anthropologic nature.

122. Spencer, Joab. "Missouri's Aboriginal Inhabitants,"
Missouri Historical Review 3 (January 1909): 275-
292, and 4 (October 1909): 18-28.

Consists of fairly brief enthnohistorical sketches
of the state's tribes, including the Osage. The
second part deals with manners, customs, and habits
and describes Osage marriage, mourning, and an
1868 honor dance.

123. Swan, Daniel. "Spatial Patterns in Osage Homestead
Selections: A Preliminary Analysis of the Relation-
ship Between Band and Village in Osage Socio-
Political History," in John H. Moore, editor, Spe-
cial Volume, "Ethnology in Oklahoma," Papers in
Anthropology 21 (Fall 1980): 77-91.

In an interesting study which raises as many
questions as it answers, the author demonstrates
through statistical analysis that the Osages tended
to choose their homesteads in the allotment selection largely according to established band and village living arrangements.

124. Terrell, John Upton. Sioux Trail. New York: Mc-
Graw-Hill Book Company, 1974. 213 pp.

Includes one chapter specifically on the Osages,
offering a simple cultural and historical overview
relying heavily on John Joseph Mathews and other
printed sources.

125- Terrell, John Upton, and Donna M. Terrell. Indian
26.   Women of the Western Morning: Their Life in
Early America. New York: The Dial Press, 1974.
214 pp.

The Osages are mentioned most prominently in
relation to the tribe's origin account.

127. Thompson, Stith. Tales of the North American Indians.
      Cambridge: Harvard University Press, 1929. 386
      pp.

          This collection contains one Osage story, "The
          Fatal Swing."

128. Velie, Alan R., editor. American Indian Literature,
      An Anthology. Norman: University of Oklahoma
      Press, 1979. 356 pp.

          Included are an excerpt from Osage writer John
          Joseph Mathews' Wah'Kon-Tah and poems by Osage
          poet Carter Revard.

129. Voget, Fred W. Osage Research Report, in Osage In-
      dians. New York: Garland Publishing Inc., 1974.
      Garland American Indian Ethnohistory Series. Vol-
      ume I, 371 pp.

          Compiled from primary sources, this account
          offers an ethnohistorical narrative of the Osages
          from the seventeenth century through the first quarter
          of the nineteenth century.

129a. Williams, Alfred M. "The Giants of the Plains,"
       Lippincott's Monthly, n. 5. 6 (1883): 362-371.

          Describes some aspects of Osage ceremonialism
          during his visit with the tribe.

130. Wilson, Lillian Ella. "Old Osage Religion Is Similar
      to Ancient Jewish Faith," The American Indian
      (Tulsa, Oklahoma) 3 (1928): 14.

          Some writers and observers of the American
          Indian could never quite rid themselves of the no-
          tion that the Native American was descended from
          the lost tribes of Israel.

131. Wolff, Hans Felix. "An Osage Graphemic Experiment,"
      International Journal of American Linguistics 24
      (June 1958): 30-35.

132. Wolff, Hans Felix. "Osage I: Phonemes and Historical
      Phonology," International Journal of American Lin-
      guistics 18 (October 1952): 63-68; "II: Morphology,"
      231-237.

133. Youngman, Reverend W. E.   Gleanings from the West-
      ern Prairies.   Cambridge, England, n.p. , 1882.

      Contains some observations of Osage customs
      and camp life.

134.   Abel, Annie Heloise. "Indian Reservations in Kansas and the Extinguishment of Their Title," Transactions of the Kansas State Historical Society 8 (1903-1904): 72-109.

An account of the removal of the Osages and other tribes from Kansas emphasizing the political background at the national and state level.

135.   Abel, Annie Heloise. "Indians in the Civil War," American Historical Review 15 (January 1910): 281-296.

Mostly concerned with the Five Civilized Tribes, but the Osages are also considered.

136.   Abel, Annie Heloise. The American Indian as Slaveholder and Secessionist. Cleveland: The Arthur H. Clark Company, 1919. 394 pp.

The Osages are included in Abel's classic study with some relevant correspondence quoted verbatim.

137.   Abel, Annie Heloise. The American Indian Under Reconstruction. Cleveland: The Arthur H. Clark Company, 1925. Reprinted by the Johnson Reprint Corporation, 1970. 419 pp.

The Osages are briefly treated in this classic study.

138.   Abel, Annie Heloise. "The History of Events Resulting

in Indian Consolidation West of the Mississippi,"
in the American Historical Association Annual Report, 1906. Volume I. Washington, D. C. , 1908,
pp. 233-454. Reprinted by the AMS Press, New
York, 1972.

Includes an account of the 1820s' negotiations by
the U. S. to get the Osages and Kansas to cede their
trans-Missouri hunting grounds.

139. Adair, E. R. "Anglo-French Rivalry in the Fur Trade
during the Eighteenth Century," Culture 8 (1947):
434-455.

The two colonial powers both desired close relations with the Osages, whose fur trade was the
most lucrative and whose proximity to the Missouri
river system made it more accessible than that of
other tribes.

140. Agnew, Brad. Fort Gibson: Terminal on the Trail of
Tears. Norman: University of Oklahoma Press,
1980. 274 pp.

Fort Gibson, established in 1824, was supposed
to keep the peace between the Cherokees and Osages, who were warring in an area where the U. S.
wanted to remove eastern tribes. The first half of
this well-researched book offers an excellent analysis of the Cherokee-Osage strife.

141. Agnew, Brad. "The Cherokee Struggle for Lovely's
Purchase," American Indian Quarterly 2 (Winter
1975-76): 347-361.

Excellent article about William Lovely's attempt
to bring peace to the warring Osages and Cherokees
in 1816 and the aftermath of his effort.

142. Allsop, Fred W. Albert Pike: A Biography. Little
Rock, Ark. : Parke-Harper Co. , 1928.

Pike negotiated treaties with the Osages and other
tribes for the Confederate States of America.

143. American State Papers, Indian Affairs. 2 vols. Wash-
      ington, D. C. : Government Printing Office, 1832-
      1834.

144. Andreu Ocariz, Juan José. Penetración española entre
      los indios Osages. Cuadernos de Filosofía y Letras,
      Serie I, Número 52. Zaragosa, 1964.

          Based on Spanish archives, this study deals with
      the Spanish encroachment on Osage territory and
      relations between the two groups of people.

145. Anson, Bert. "Variations of the Indian Conflict: The
      Effects of the Emigrant Indian Removal Policy,
      1830-1854," Missouri Historical Review 59 (October
      1964): 64-89.

          A thoughtful piece on conflicts between the Osages
      and other western tribes with southeastern Indians
      forced west.

146. Bailey, Garrick Alan. Changes in Osage Social Organ-
      ization, 1673-1906. University of Oregon Anthro-
      pological Papers, No. 5. Eugene, Oregon, 1973.
      122 pp.

          One of the most valuable works on the tribe based
      on field research and government documents.

147. Bailey, Garrick Alan. "Changes in Osage Social Or-
      ganization, 1673-1969." Ph. D. dissertation, Uni-
      versity of Oregon, 1970.

          Emphasizes the effects of white contacts on Osage
      custom leading to the disappearance of a carefully
      balanced social system.

148. Bailey, Garrick Alan. "Osage Economic and Territorial
      Change, 1673-1839." MA thesis, University of Ore-
      gon, 1968.

          Well-researched with an emphasis on change in

the internal and cultural life of the Osages resulting
from the altered economic and territorial status of
the tribe stemming from contact with the Spanish,
French, and English.

149. Baird, W. David. The Osage People.   Phoenix: In-
      dian Tribal Series, 1972.   104 pp.

          A very readable historical survey of the Osages
      enhanced by several excellent photographs, some in
      color.

150. Baird, W. David. The Quapaw Indians: A History of
      the Downstream People.   Norman: University of
      Oklahoma Press, 1980.

          Linguistically and culturally related, the Quapaws'
      history frequently mingled with that of the Osages.

151. Baptismal Records of the Osage Nation, 1820 to July
      31, 1843.   Typescript in the Missouri Historical
      Society, Saint Louis, Missouri.   The original is in
      St. Mary's, Kansas.

152. Barnes, Lela, editor.   "An Editor Looks at Early-
      Day Kansas: The Letters of Charles Monroe Chase,"
      The Kansas Historical Quarterly 26 (Summer 1960):
      113-151.

          There is one reference to the Osages from the
      1860s period in Kansas with some good description
      of a treaty party and Father Schoenmakers.

153. Barnes, Lela. "Journal of Isaac McCoy for the Ex-
      ploring Expedition of 1828." The Kansas Historical
      Quarterly 5 (August 1936): 227-277.

          McCoy, a Baptist missionary appointed commis-
      sioner to accompany eastern tribes looking for new
      homes in the west in 1828, offers good descriptions
      of Osages he encountered.

154. Barney, Ralph A. Laws Relating to the Osage Tribe
      of Indians. Pawhuska, Okla.: The Osage Printery,
      Publishers, 1929.

           Contains every piece of federal legislation per-
      taining to the Osages. Copies available from the
      Osage Superintendency have more recent laws stapled
      to the back cover.

155. Barry, Louise, compiler. "Kansas Before 1854: A
      Revised Annals," The Kansas Historical Quarterly
      27 (Spring-Summer-Autumn-Winter 1961): 67-93,
      201-219, 353-382, 497-543 and 28; (Spring-Summer-
      Autumn-Winter 1962): 317-369, 497-514, 25-59,
      167-204 and 29; (Spring-Summer-Autumn-Winter
      1963): 41-81, 143-189, 324-359, 429-486 and 30;
      (Spring-Summer-Autumn-Winter 1964): 62-91, 209-
      244, 339-412, 492-559 and 31; (Summer-Autumn
      1965): 138-199, 256-339 and 32; (Spring-Summer-
      Winter): 33-112, 210-282, 426-503.

           This mostly year-by-year compendium of major
      events in Kansas history beginning in 1540 first
      mentions the Osages in 1693 and includes mention
      of the tribe in several places. The events are
      taken from a wide variety of other writers' works.

156. Barry, Louise. The Beginning of the West: Annals
      of the Kansas Gateway to the American West, 1540-
      1854. Topeka: Kansas State Historical Society,
      1972. 1,296 pp.

           Scores of references to the Osages in this ex-
      tremely useful annals arranged chronologically by
      year.

157. Bartles, W. L. "Massacre of Confederates by Osage
      Indians in 1863," Transactions of the Kansas State
      Historical Society 8 (1903-1904): 62-66.

           Fairly straightforward account of an 1863 clash
      between Osages and Confederate troops numbering
      about 20 in Kansas on tribal land.

158. Bearss, Edwin C. "In Quest of Peace on the Indian
      Border: The Establishment of Fort Smith," The
      Arkansas Historical Quarterly 23 (Summer 1964):
      123-153.

          An excellent account of the hostilities between
      the Osages and Cherokees during the second decade
      of the nineteenth century and the subsequent erection
      of Fort Smith to help keep the peace.

159. Bearss, Edwin, and Arrell M. Gibson. Fort Smith:
      Little Gibraltar on the Arkansas. Norman: Uni-
      versity of Oklahoma Press, 1969.

          This well-documented study includes much of in-
      terest concerning the Osages, especially their war
      with the Cherokees that was ended by a treaty ne-
      gotiated at Ft. Smith.

160. Becknell, Captain William. "Journals from Boone's
      Lick to Santa Fe, and from Santa Cruz to Green
      River," Missouri Historical Review 4 (January 1910):
      65-84.

          Mostly uncomplimentary references to the Osages
      in these excerpts from an 1821 journey concerning
      thievery.

161. Beckwith, H. W. "Hennepin's Narrative from His 'La
      Louisiane' of 1683," Collections of the Illinois State
      Historical Library 1 (1903): 46-105.

          Hennepin encountered Osages on his river journey.

162. Beerman, Eric. "XV Baron de Carondelet, Gobernador
      de la Luisiana y la Florida (1791-1797)," Hidalguía
      (1978): 3-15.

          Carondelet as governor of Louisiana was anxious
      to forge an alliance with the powerful Osages.

163. Billington, Ray Allen, and Martin Ridge. Westward

Expansion: A History of the American Frontier.
New York: Macmillan Publishing Co. , 1982. 892
pp.

One of the best standard surveys of the history
of the west.

164.   Blackburn, Bob L. "First Lieutenant James B. Wilk-
inson, 1806-1807," in Joseph A. Stout, Jr. , editor,
Frontier Adventurers: American Exploration in
Oklahoma. Oklahoma City: Oklahoma Historical
Society, 1976, pp. 6-19.

Wilkinson visited the Osages on the Missouri.
He was under orders to "pacify" and gain an alliance and trade agreement with them.

165.   Boas, Franz. "Census of the North American Indians."
Publications of the American Economic Association.
n. s. 2 (March 1899): 49-53.

166.   Bourassa, J. N. "The Life of Wah-Bahn-Se: The
Warrior Chief of the Pottawatamies," The Kansas
Historical Quarterly 38 (Summer 1972): 132-141.

Contains a few pages on the Potawatomi chief's
battles with the Osages and his adoption of an Osage
boy.

167.   Brackenridge, Henry Marie. Journal of a Voyage up
the River Missouri, Performed in Eighteen Hundred
and Eleven. 2nd edition. Baltimore, 1816. Reprinted in Reuben Gold Thwaites, editor, Early
Western Travels, 1748-1846. Volume VI. Cleveland: Arthur H. Clark Company, 1904-1907.

Much quoted by later scholars, Brackenridge's
detailed observations of the Osages after his 1811
visit were marred by his excessive ethnocentrism,
which blinded him to the actual motivations behind
many tribal customs. Probably he was disappointed
in the relatively "ignoble savage" he found when ex-
pecting a poetically pristine state of nature.

168.   Bradbury, John. Travels in the Interior of America,
        1809-1811. 2nd edition. London, 1819. Reprinted
        in Reuben Gold Thwaites, editor, Early Western
        Travels, 1748-1846. Volume V. Cleveland: Arthur
        H. Clark Company, 1904-1907.

            Interested in geology and botany, Bradbury made
        careful observations of the Osage country as well
        as the Osages and recorded many of the tribal ways,
        unfortunately not always ascribing the correct rea-
        sons and motivations for their form.

169.   Brazelton, Audra Neil. "Family Life of the Osage In-
        dians Previous to 1872." MA thesis, University
        of Missouri, 1935.

170.   Brewster, S. W. "Reverend Father Paul M. Ponzig-
        lione," The Transactions of the Kansas State His-
        torical Society 9 (1905-1908): 19-32.

            Father Ponziglione was second only to Father
        Schoenmakers at the Osage Mission in Kansas dur-
        ing the 1850s and 1860s.

171.   Broadhead, Garland C. "Harmony Mission and Metho-
        dist Missions," Missouri Historical Review 9 (Jan-
        uary 1915): 102-103.

            Tells of an 1820 Osage delegation in Washington
        requesting missionaries and the Methodist response.

172.   Broadhead, Garland C. "The Santa Fe Trail," Missouri
        Historical Review 4 (July 1910): 309-319.

            The Osages are mentioned prominently in this
        brief glance at famous travelers using the Santa
        Fe Trail.

173.   Brooks, George R. , editor. "George C. Sibley's Jour-
        nal of a Trip to the Salines in 1811," Bulletin of
        the Missouri Historical Society 59 (April 1965):
        171-208.

Sibley was guided by Osages on his journey to find salt and visited chief Clermont's hunting camp in eastern Oklahoma.

174. Brophy, Patrick. "Pawhuska: Unsung Hero of the Osages," Missouri Life (March-April 1978): 48-52.

Enhanced by several excellent quality color photographs by the author, this piece offers a biographical sketch of Pawhuska, a prominent Osage chief of the early 1800s, placing him in the context of tribal and U. S. history.

175. Buchanan, James. Sketches of the History, Manners, and Customs of the North American Indians. London: Black, Young & Young, 1824.

Includes some firsthand accounts of the Osages.

176. Burns, Louis F. "Old Trails Across Northern Osage County," The Chronicles of Oklahoma 59 (Winter 1981-1982): 422-429.

Describes old Osage and other Indian trails.

177. Busby, Orel. "Buffalo Valley: An Osage Hunting Ground," The Chronicles of Oklahoma 40 (Spring 1962): 22-35.

Located in Pototoc County, Buffalo Valley was an Osage hunting area frequented by Black Dog's band.

178. Caldwell, Martha B. "The Southern Kansas Boundary Survey: From the Journal of Hugh Campbell, Astronomical Computer," The Kansas Historical Quarterly 6 (November 1937).

Contains an excellent description of a mounted Osage hunting party in 1857.

179. Carman, J. Neale. "The Bishop East of the Rockies
      Views His Diocesans, 1851-1853," The Kansas His-
      torical Quarterly 21 (Summer 1954): 81-86.

          Offers excerpts from Bishop Jean-Baptiste Miège's
      letters on the condition of the Potawatomi and Osage
      Indians.

180. Carriker, Robert C. Fort Supply, Indian Territory:
      Frontier Outpost on the Plains. Norman: Univer-
      sity of Oklahoma Press, 1970. 241 pp.

          The Osages figure largely in this study of a
      southern plains military post.

181. Carter, Clarence E. , editor. Territorial Papers of
      the United States. 26 vols. Washington, D. C. :
      Government Printing Office, 1934-1962.

182. Caruso, John Anthony. The Mississippi Valley Frontier:
      The Age of French Exploration and Settlement.
      Indianapolis: The Bobbs-Merrill Co. , Inc. , 1966.
      423 pp.

          The author has included an entire chapter on
      the Osages and the French.

183. Case, Nelson. History of Labette County, Kansas.
      Topeka: Crane and Company, 1893.

          This county was one created from territory ceded
      by the Osages in the late 1860s.

184. Castel, Albert, E. Frontier State at War: Kansas,
      1861-1865. Ithaca, N. Y. : Cornell University
      Press, 1958. 251 pp.

          The Osages are dealt with rather briefly along
      with other tribes in the state during the Civil War.

185. Chapman, Berlin B. "Charles Curtis and the Kaw

Reservation," The Kansas Historical Quarterly 15 (November 1947): 337-352.

The Kaw reservation was carved out of Osage land and the two tribes shared a single agent in Indian Territory after 1873.

186. Chapman, Berlin B. "How the Cherokees Acquired and Disposed of the Outlet," The Chronicles of Oklahoma 15 (March-June-September 1937): 30-49, 204-225, 291-321; 16 (March-June 1938): 36-51, 135-162.

The Cherokees won part of their Indian Territory land from the Osages, who later purchased a portion of it back for a reservation in 1871.

187. Chapman, Berlin B. "Removal of the Osages from Kansas," Kansas Historical Quarterly 7 (August 1938): 287-305; 7 (November 1938): 399-410.

A two-part article that is the best published account of this event, which occurred in 1871, but whose antecedents stretched back to 1858.

188. Chapman, Carl Haley. "The Indomitable Osage in Spanish Illinois (Upper Louisiana) 1763-1804," in John Francis McDermott, editor, Spain in the Mississippi Valley, 1762-1804. Urbana: University of Illinois Press, 1974, pp. 187-312.

Good description of Osage villages, hunting activities, political organization, and warfare.

189. Chappell, Phil E. "A History of the Missouri River," Transactions of the Kansas State Historical Society 9 (1905-1906): 237-294.

Devotes several pages to the Osages, quoting extensively from primary documents.

190. Chepesiuk, Ron, and Arnold Shankman, compilers.

American Indian Archival Material: A Guide to
Holdings in the Southeast. Westport, Conn.: Green-
wood Press, 1982. 325 pp.

Contains references to about a dozen archival
collections that include Osage material.

191. Christianson, James R. "A Study of Osage History
Prior to 1876." Ph.D. dissertation, University of
Kansas, 1968.

Especially good for the period of the Osages on
their Kansas reservation, a study marked by thorough
research.

192. Clark, Ira G. "The Railroads and the Tribal Lands:
Indian Territory, 1838-1890." Ph.D. dissertation,
University of California, Berkeley, 1947.

193. Clarke, Sidney. Remonstrance Against the Treaty with
the Great and Little Osage Indians. Washington,
D.C.: Gibson Brothers, Printers, 1868.

Kansas Senator Sidney Clarke had his address
before the U.S. Senate printed and distributed in
pamphlet form. It attacked the Drum Creek treaty
negotiations of 1868, correctly, as an attempted land
grab by railroad interests.

194. Collot, George Henry Victery. A Journey in North
America. 2 vols. Paris, 1826. Reprinted in
1924 in Florence.

Collot's travels, which included a visit to the
Osages, were seen as spying for French colonial
aspirations by the Spanish.

195. Conard, Howard L., editor. Encyclopedia of the History of Missouri. 6 vols. New York: Scribners,
1901.

196. Connelly, William E. A Standard History of Kansas
      and Kansans. 5 vols. New York: Arthur H. Clark,
      1918.

          Includes excellent coverage of the Indian aspect
          of the state's history.

197. Coonrod, Guy R. "Kansas Indian Lands, 1803-1854."
      MA thesis, University of Colorado, 1947.

198. Cornelius, Elias. The Little Osage Captive: An Au-
      thentic Narrative. York, England: W. Alexander
      & Son, 1821. 182 pp.

          Offers an account of an Osage girl captured by
          the Cherokees and rescued by the author, who named
          her Lydia Carter.

199. Cortambert, Louis. "Journey to the Land of the Osages,
      1835-1836," Bulletin of the Missouri Historical So-
      ciety 19 (April 1963): 199-229.

          Translated by Mrs. Max W. Myer and edited by
          Carl H. Chapman, this reprinting of the original
          1837 book, a rare item, contains much less detail
          on Osage life than the title would indicate.

200. Cortambert, Louis. Voyage au pays des Osages.
      Paris: A. Bertrand, 1837.

          Disappointing for its inattention to detail of In-
          dian life such as that provided by travelers of the
          same period, like Victor Tixier.

201. Cory, C. E. "The Osage Ceded Lands," Transactions
      of the Kansas State Historical Society 8 (1903-1904):
      187-199.

          Juxtaposes the white settlers and Osages contest-
          ing control over the eastern part of the Kansas
          reservation in the 1860s.

202.   Coues, Elliot, editor. The Expeditions of Zebulon
        Montgomery Pike. 3 vols. New York: F. P.
        Harper, 1895.

            Pike's 1805-1807 expedition of exploration and
        diplomacy began with a return of Osage prisoners
        among the Potawatomis to the tribe and members
        of the tribe accompanied him on his travels west.

203.   Coues, Elliot, editor. The Journal of Jacob Fowler,
        1821-22. New York, 1898. Reprinted in 1970 by
        the University of Nebraska Press, Lincoln.

            A junior partner of Hugh Glenn on an 1821 jour-
        ney from Missouri to Santa Fe, Fowler kept a de-
        tailed diary which included some material on the
        Osages who were encamped in present Oklahoma
        for their fall buffalo hunt.

204.   Cox, Osaac J. "The Exploration of the Louisiana
        Frontier, 1803-1806," in American Historical As-
        sociation Annual Report, 1904. Washington, D.C.,
        1905, pp. 151-174.

            Several explorers came into contact with the
        Osages during this period, including Lt. James
        Wilkinson and Zebulon Pike.

205.   Crawford, Samuel J. Kansas in the Sixties. Chicago:
        A. C. McClurg & Co., 1911. 441 pp.

            Written by a former governor of Kansas in the
        1860s, this narrative offers a chapter on Indian
        land frauds, including the 1868 Osage treaty. Sev-
        eral primary documents are quoted in full or at
        length.

206.   Cunningham, Frank. General Stand Watie's Confeder-
        ate Indians. San Antonio, Texas: The Naylor Com-
        pany, 1959. 239 pp.

            Although focused on the Confederate Indians,
        this study contains several references to the Os-
        ages fighting for the Union.

207. Custer, George Armstrong. My Life on the Plains
      or, Personal Experiences with Indians. Introduc-
      tion by Edgar I. Stewart. Norman: University of
      Oklahoma Press, 1962. 418 pp.

      Several references are made to the Osage scouts,
      led by Hard Rope and Little Beaver, who accom-
      panied Custer on his 1867-68 campaign.

208. Debo, Angie. The Road to Disappearance. Norman:
      University of Oklahoma Press, 1941. 399 pp.

      This history of the Creek tribe contains good
      accounts of encounters, mostly hostile, with the
      Osages.

209. Delaunay, D. The Osage Indians ... 1827. Bartles-
      ville, Okla. : Motter Bindery, 1940.

210. Denton, Doris. "Harmony Mission, 1821-1837." MA
      thesis, University of Kansas, 1929.

      This was the first Protestant missionary activity
      among the Osages.

211. De Smet, Rev. P. J. Western Missions and Mission-
      aries: A Series of Letters. New York: Catholic
      Publishing House, 1859. 532 pp.

      Includes four lengthy and descriptive letters from
      Father F. Bax written during the early 1850s about
      the Osage mission and one from Father De Smet
      describing Bax's work among the Osages.

212. Din, Gilbert C. "Arkansas Post in the American Revo-
      lution," Arkansas Historical Quarterly 60 (Spring
      1981): 3-30.

      In 1777 the Osages and Quapaws discussed a
      peace with the Spanish at the Arkansas Post.

213. Din, Gilbert C. "Protecting the 'Barrera': Spain's

Defenses in Louisiana, 1763-1779," Louisiana History 19 (Spring 1978): 183-211.

It was during this period that the Spanish first made contact with the Osages, a tribe that had to be courted to maintain Spain's position in Louisiana.

214. Din, Gilbert C., and Abraham P. Nasatir. The Imperial Osages: Spanish-Indian Diplomacy in the Mississippi Valley. Norman: University of Oklahoma Press, 1983. 432 pp.

Based on exhaustive research, especially in Spanish archival collections, this work is the definitive study of the Osages and their relations with the Spanish and French; unfortunately it contains less of the tribe's perspective than that of the European powers.

215. Dodge, Reverend Nathaniel. "Annual Report," Missionary Herald 27 (1831): 288-289.

Dodge and other Protestant missionaries gamely continued their largely futile efforts to "civilize" the Osages.

216. Dodge, Reverend Nathaniel. "Harmony," Missionary Herald 23 (1827): 149-150.

Harmony was a Protestant mission to the Osages.

217. Donohue, Arthur T. "A History of the Early Jesuit Missions in Kansas," Ph.D. dissertation. University of Kansas, 1932.

218. Douglas, Walter Bond. "Captain Nathaniel Pryor," American Historical Review 24 (January 1919): 253-265.

Pryor, an Indian trader, became an intermarried citizen of the Osage tribe and was very influential in decision-making regarding relations with the U.S. between 1815 and 1825.

219. Douglas, Walter Bond. Manuel Lisa. Annotated and
      edited by Abraham P. Nasatir. New York: Argosy
      Antiquarian, 1964. 207 pp.

      Manuel Lisa, a Spaniard, received exclusive
      rights of trade with the Osages from the Governor-
      General of Louisiana in 1802 and played a power-
      ful role in tribal affairs for several years there-
      after.

220. Douglas, Walter Bond. "Manuel Lisa," Missouri His-
      torical Society Collections 3 (1911): 233-268 and 4
      (1911): 367-406.

      Relates how Lisa, a Spanish fur trader, worked
      to wrest the Osage trade from the Chouteaus.

221. Douglas, Walter Bond. "The Sieurs de St. Ange,"
      Transactions of the Illinois State Historical Society,
      1909, pp. 135-146.

      St. Ange was an advisor to Louisiana Governor
      Antonio de Ulloa in his formulations of Indian policy
      in the 1760s. He urged the courting of the Osages'
      friendship rather than an aggressive stance toward
      the tribe.

222. Duncan, Lew Wallace. History of Neosho and Wilson
      Counties, Kansas. Fort Scott, Han.: Monitor
      Printing Company, 1902. 922 pp.

      Several Osage villages and the Union Mission
      were located in what later became Neosho County.

223. Eaton, David W., contributor. "Harmony Mission:
      Morse's Report on Indian Affairs," Missouri His-
      torical Review 9 (April 1915): 183-191.

      Has excerpts from several missionaries' letters
      about the progress of Harmony Mission among the
      Osages in 1821 and 1822.

224. Eaton, Rachel Caroline. "The Legend of the Battle of

Claremore Mound," The Chronicles of Oklahoma 8
(December 1930): 369-377.

A good description of the background and actual
battle of Claremore Mound where Cherokees, their
Indian allies, and a handful of white men destroyed
an Osage village in two days of fighting in 1819.

225. Edmunds, R. David. The Potawatomis: Keepers of
      the Fire. Norman: University of Oklahoma Press,
      362 pp.

      Includes some thoughtful discussion of hostilities
      between the Osages and Potawatomis in the 1790s.

226. Elliott, William B. "A Study of the Removal of the
      Osage Indians from Missouri to Indian Territory,"
      MS thesis, Kansas State College of Pittsburg, 1941.

227. Evans, Charles. Lights on Oklahoma History. Okla-
      homa City: Harlow Publishing Company, 1920.
      187 pp.

      Among several historical sketches are accounts
      of the Battle of Claremore Mound between the Osages
      and Cherokees and Washington Irving's tour of the
      prairies.

228. Every, Dale Van. The Final Challenge: The American
      Frontier, 1804-1845. New York: William Morrow
      and Company, 1964. 378 pp.

      Has some interesting characterizations of the
      Osages as a people and tribe.

229. Faye, Stanley. "The Arkansas Post of Louisiana:
      French Dominion," Louisiana Historical Quarterly
      26 (July 1943): 633-721.

      This was a major trading and military station
      that played an important role in French-Osage af-
      fairs.

230.   Fessler, W. Julian. "Captain Nathan Boone's Journal,"
        The Chronicles of Oklahoma 7 (March 1929): 58-
        105.

              Boone, the youngest son of Daniel Boone, led
        an expedition of U.S. dragoons in 1843 into Indian
        Territory from Fort Gibson encountering Osages
        who stole horses from him.

231.   Fitzgerald, Sister Mary Paul. Beacon on the Plains.
        Leavenworth, Kan.: The Saint Mary College, 1939.
        297 pp.

              Very well researched account of the Catholic
        mission to the Osages in Kansas.

232.   Fitzgerald, Sister Mary Paul. "John Baptist Miège,
        S. J., 1815-1884, First Vicar Apostolic of the In-
        dian Territory: A Study in Frontier History," His-
        torical Records and Studies 24 (1934): 284-362.

              Miège and Father Paul Ponziglione visited Indian
        Territory together and planned the Jesuit mission
        for the Osages.

233.   Fitzgerald, Sister Mary Paul. "Osage Mission, a Fac-
        tor in the Making of Kansas," Mid-America 19 (July
        1937): 182-196.

              A distillation of the author's thesis on the Jesuit
        mission among the Osages in Kansas.

234.   Fitzgerald, Sister Mary Paul. "The Osage Missions:
        A Factor in the Making of Kansas." MA thesis,
        St. Louis University, 1936.

              An excellent thesis that documents the labors of
        Catholic missionaries among the Osages until the
        tribe's departure in 1871, and includes a good ac-
        count of the Jesuit fathers' involvement in tribal
        and local Kansas politics.

235.   Fitzgerald, Sister Mary Paul. "The Osage Mission:

A Factor in the Making of Kansas." Ph. D. dissertation, St. Louis University, 1936.

Deals with the Jesuit-run mission among the
Osages up to the time of the tribe's departure from
Kansas in 1871.

236. Fletcher, A. C. "Osage Indians in France," American
Anthropologist 2 (1900): 395-400.

A brief comment on the trip made by a group
of Osages to France in the 1820s.

237. Foley, William E. A History of Missouri, 1673 to
1820. Columbia: University of Missouri Press,
1971. 237 pp.

The first of a five-volume collection work, this
history features the Osages prominently.

238. Foley, William E. "Compounding the Risks: International Politics, War Time Dislocations, and Auguste
Chouteau's Fur Trading Operations 1792-1815,"
Missouri Historical Society Bulletin 34 (April 1978):
131-139.

The Osages were the object of much commercial
and political attention from Chouteau's during this
turbulent period, during part of which they had a
monopoly on the tribe's trade.

239. Foley, William E. "James A. Wilkinson: Territorial
Governor," Missouri Historical Society Bulletin 26
(October 1968): 1-17.

Wilkinson sent his own son, an army officer, to
explore the Arkansas River in 1807 and to bear
messages for the Osages.

240. Foley, William E. "The Lewis and Clark Expedition's
Silent Partners: The Chouteau Brothers of St. Louis,"
Missouri Historical Review 77 (January 1983): 131-
146.

Gives an excellent account of Pierre Chouteau's party of Osages taken to Washington in 1804.

241. Foley, William E. , and Charles David Rice. "Pierre Chouteau, Entrepreneur as Indian Agent," Missouri Historical Review 72 (July 1978): 365-387.

Chouteau, with his brother a fur trader before the U. S. purchased Louisiana, was appointed the first American Indian agent to the Osages.

242. Foreman, Carolyn Thomas. "Education Among the Quapaws, 1829-1875," The Chronicles of Oklahoma 25 (Spring 1947): 15-29.

The education of the Quapaws was tied to that of the Osages as the two tribes were partially merged during this period.

243. Foreman, Carolyn Thomas. "Hopefield Mission in Osage Nation, 1823-1837," The Chronicles of Oklahoma 28 (Summer 1950): 193-205.

Established on the Neosho River in Kansas, the Hopefield Mission did not thrive as an agricultural example due to sickness among the missionaries and Indians as well as bad weather and plagues of insects.

244. Foreman, Carolyn Thomas. Indians Abroad, 1493-1938. Norman: University of Oklahoma Press, 1943. 247pp.

One entire chapter is devoted to the visit of 25 Osages to Europe in 1827 and there are also some brief notes on Osage doughboys in World War I.

245. Foreman, Carolyn Thomas. "Nathan Boone: Trapper, Manufacturer, Surveyor, Militiaman, Legislator, Ranger, and Dragoon," The Chronicles of Oklahoma 19 (December 1941): 322-345.

Boone's life intersected with that of the Osages
in 1808 when he helped pressure them from Missouri and later in 1843 when he reluctantly used
them for guides in a search for the salt plains of
eastern Oklahoma.

246.   Foreman, Grant. Advancing the Frontier, 1830-1860.
        Norman: University of Oklahoma Press, 1933.
        363pp.

        Particularly good in discussions of the different
        councils arising out of conflicts between emigrant
        and resident tribes of Indian Territory.

247.   Foreman, Grant. Fort Gibson: A Brief History.
        Norman: University of Oklahoma Press, 1936.

        Fort Gibson's early history was closely tied to
        that of the Osages.

248.   Foreman, Grant. Indians and Pioneers: The Story
        of the American Southwest before 1830. New Haven:
        Yale University Press, 1930.   348 pp.

        Offers a detailed account of the bitter warfare
        between the Osages and Cherokees.   This is the
        best source on this period of the tribe's history.

249.   Foreman, Grant. "Nathaniel Pryor," The Chronicles
        of Oklahoma 7 (June 1929): 152-163.

        This is a biographical sketch of Pryor who was
        a subagent of the U. S. government to the Osages
        just prior to his death in 1831.   For several years
        previously he lived with the tribe and served as a
        negotiator for them on numerous occasions.

250.   Foreman, Grant. "Our Indian Ambassadours to Eu-
        rope," Missouri Historical Society Collections 5
        (February 1928): 109-128.

        With several interesting reproductions of paint-

ings, this piece describes the experiences of an
1827 party of Osages who visited Europe for three
years.

251.   Foreman, Grant. "Salt Works in Early Oklahoma,"
        The Chronicles of Oklahoma 10 (December 1932):
        474-500.

        The first part of this article deals with an east-
        ern Oklahoma salt spring and deposit located near
        a large Osage village that figured importantly in
        the tribe's history.

252.   Foreman, Grant. "The Centennial of Fort Gibson,"
        The Chronicles of Oklahoma 2 (June 1924): 119-
        128.

        Fort Gibson was founded in 1824 to keep the
        peace between the Osages and Cherokees.   Fore-
        man draws some ironic parallels with that time and
        the 1920s' wealthy Osages.

253.   Foreman, Grant. "The Journal of the Proceedings of
        Our First Treaty with the Wild Indians, 1835,"
        The Chronicles of Oklahoma 14 (December 1936):
        393-418.

        The Osages were among the tribes attending the
        1835 treaty negotiations conducted by Governor Mont-
        fort Stokes and General M. Arbuckle.

254.   Foreman, Grant. The Last Trek of the Indians.   Chi-
        cago: University of Chicago Press, 1946.   382 pp.

        The author devotes an entire chapter to the Osage
        and Kaw (Kansa) tribes describing the major his-
        torical events of their reservation life in Kansas
        and later Oklahoma Territory.

255.   Foreman, Grant. "Three Forks," The Chronicles of
        Oklahoma 2 (March 1924): 37-47.

The junction of the three forks of the Arkansas River in Oklahoma was the site of a village of Osages headed originally by Cashesegra, who was convinced to move there by the Chouteau Indian traders.

256.   Forrest, Herbert J. "Malaria and the Union Mission to the Osage Indians, 1820-1837," Oklahoma State Medical Association Journal 69 (July 1976): 322-327.

257.   Friehrer, Thomas M. "The Baron de Carondelet as Agent of Bourbon Reform." Ph. D. dissertation, Tulane University, 1977.

Carondelet was governor of Louisiana from 1792 to 1798. He dealt with the Osages extensively and a fort bearing his name was erected among them to control their hostility.

258.   Gabler, Ina. "Lovely's Purchase and Lovely County," The Arkansas Historical Quarterly 19 (Spring 1960): 31-39.

Offers a brief account of the 1816-18 imbroglio between the Osages and Cherokees over the contradictory tribal cessions of land engineered in part by Major William Lovely, Cherokee agent in Missouri Territory. Includes two excellent maps.

259.   Garfield, Marvin H. "Defense of the Kansas Frontier 1868-1869," The Kansas Historical Quarterly 1 (November 1932): 451-473.

The Osages were among the tribes committing depredations.

260.   Garraghan, Gilbert J. "Fort Orleans on the Missouri," Missouri Historical Review 35 (April 1941): 373-384.

Built by the French in 1723, Fort Orleans on

the north bank of the Missouri River was an important post in Osage territory.

261. Garraghan, Gilbert J. , S. J.   The Jesuits of the Middle
     United States.   3 volumes.   New York: America
     Press, 1938.

     Offers an extensive history of the Kansas Osage
     mission in present Neosho County from the 1820s
     to the early 1870s.

262. Gates, Paul Wallace.   Fifty Million Acres: Conflicts
     over Kansas Land Policy, 1854-1890.   Ithaca, N. Y. :
     Cornell University Press, 1954.   311 pp.

     An entire chapter of this excellently researched
     work deals with the struggle over the Osage re-
     serve, the last Indian land left in Kansas.

263. Gibson, A. M.   The Kickapoos: Lords of the Middle
     Border.   Norman: University of Oklahoma Press,
     1963.   387 pp.

     This well-written study has numerous references
     to the Osages, who were constant enemies of the
     Kickapoos.

264. Gibson, Arrell Morgan.   The American Indian: Pre-
     history to the Present.   Lexington, Mass. :   D. C.
     Health and Company, 1980.   618 pp.

     Despite its general title, this survey is particu-
     larly strong on Oklahoma Indians, including the Os-
     ages both before and after they arrived in the state.

265. Gilbert, Grace M.   "Indian Missions of Southeastern
     Kansas," MS thesis, Kansas State Teachers' Col-
     lege, Emporia, 1936.

     The emphasis is on the Osage Mission.

266. Giles, Janice H. Johnny Osage. Boston: Houghton
      Mifflin Co. , 1960. 313 pp.

      Based on historical research at the Oklahoma
      Historical Society, the story revolves around a
      mixed-blood member of the tribe during the period
      of warfare between the Osages and Cherokees.

267. Giraud, Marcel, editor. "L'Exacte Description de la
      Louisiana, D'Etienne Véniard de Bourgmont," Revue
      Historique 217 (January-March 1957): 29-41. Trans-
      lated by Mrs. Max W. Meyer, Missouri Historical
      Society Bulletin 15 (October 1958): 3-19.

      Bourgmont, who founded Fort Orleans, was well-
      liked by the Osages and was largely responsible for
      tribe's friendly relations with France in the 1720s.

268. Gittinger, Roy. "The Separation of Nebraska and Kan-
      sas from the Indian Territory," Mississippi Valley
      Historical Review 3 (March 1917): 442-461.

      The Osage reserve was included in this land
      area and the dividing line between the tribe and
      the Cherokees was made the southern boundary of
      Kansas.

269. Glenn, Robert A. "The Osage War," Missouri Histori-
      cal Review 14 (January 1920): 201-210.

      In 1837 the Osages, surrounded by eastern tribes
      and white settlers, engaged in "warfare" with the
      citizens of Missouri over hunting rights. This ver-
      sion contains several lengthy quotations from pri-
      mary sources.

270. Godsey, Roy. "The Osage War," Missouri Historical
      Review 20 (October 1925): 96-100.

      The 1837 war between the Osages and white Mis-
      sourians over hunting rights resulted in the official
      physical division of the Arkansas band from the re-

mainder of the tribe.   This article consists chiefly
of two letters about the military aspects of the war.

271.   Goetzmann, William H.   Exploration and Empire: The
       Explorer and the Scientist in the Winning of the
       American West.   New York: Alfred A. Knopf, 1971.
       656 pp.

       Several of the explorers described in the book
       visited the Osages.

272.   Gragert, Steven.   "Thomas Nuttall, 1819," in Joseph
       A. Stout, Jr., editor, Frontier Adventurers: Amer-
       ican Exploration in Oklahoma.   Oklahoma City: Ok-
       lahoma Historical Society, 1976, pp. 38-50.

       A renowned botanist, Nuttall encountered the
       Osages on his expedition and wrote extensively about
       their appearance and customs.

273.   Grant, Bruce.   American Indians: Yesterday and To-
       day.   New York: E. P. Dutton & Co., Inc., 1958.
       349 pp.

       Has a few references to the Osages, but is not
       a very useful reference since it is not indexed.

274.   Graustein, Jeannette.   Thomas Nuttall, Naturalist:
       Explorations in America, 1808-1841.   Cambridge:
       Harvard University Press, 1967.   481 pp.

       Nuttall visited the Osages during his travels and
       describes the tribe at some length.

275.   Graves, Mrs. W. W.   "In the land of the Osages--
       Harmony Mission," Missouri Historical Review 19
       (April 1925):   409-418.

       A somewhat sentimental sketch of Harmony Mis-
       sion established in 1821, but it does have some
       lengthy quotations from primary sources.

276. Graves, William W. Annals of Osage Mission. St. Paul, Kan. : W. W. Graves, 1934.

A considerable amount of primary material reprinted in a straightforward narrative of the Kansas Jesuit-run Osage mission.

277. Graves, William W. Early Jesuits at Osage Mission. St. Paul, Kan. : W. W. Graves, 1916.

Briefly deals with the founders of the Osage mission in Kansas during the 1840s and 1850s.

278. Graves, William W. History of Neosho County. 2 vols. St. Paul, Kan. : Journal Press, 1949-1951.

Neosho County was the site of the Union Mission and several Osage villages.

279. Graves, William W. Life and Letters of Fathers Ponziglione, Schoenmakers and Other Early Jesuits of Osage Mission: Sketch of St. Francis' Church Life of Mother Bridget. 287 pp. St. Paul, Kan. : W. W. Graves, 1916.

Much otherwise nearly unobtainable correspondence published along with extensive biographical information.

280. Graves, William W. Life and Letters of Reverend Father John Schoenmakers, S. J. : Apostle to the Osages. Parsons, Kan. : The Commercial Publishers, 1928. 144 pp.

Schoenmakers was very influential in Osage affairs, religious and otherwise, in Kansas and after 1871 in Indian Territory.

281. Graves, William W. Life and Times of Mother Bridget Hayden. St. Paul, Kan. : Journal Press, 1938. 324 pp.

Mother Hayden headed the Sisters of Loretto's
mission efforts among the Osages.

282.   Graves, William W.   The Broken Treaty: A Story of
       the Osage Country.   St. Paul Kan. :   The Journal,
       1935.

       A work of historical fiction, the narrative re-
       volves around the Civil War period and the Con-
       federate-Osage treaty that was negotiated by Albert
       Pike in Kansas.

283.   Graves, William W.   The First Protestant Osage Mis-
       sions, 1820-1837.   Oswego, Kan. : Carpenter Press,
       1949.   272 pp.

       Records the activities of the Protestants among
       the Osages in Missouri at the Harmony Mission.

284.   Gregg, Josiah.   Commerce of the Prairies.   Norman:
       University of Oklahoma Press, 1954.   469 pp.

       The Osages were frequent raiders of wagon trains
       on the Santa Fe Trail and they are described in
       some detail in this classic of frontier transporta-
       tion and economic history.

285.   Gregg, Kate L.   "The History of Fort Osage," Mis-
       souri Historical Review 34 (July 1940):   439-488.

       Built in 1808 in accordance with treaty terms
       agreed upon by the U. S. and the Osages, Fort Os-
       age on the Missouri was often called Fort William
       Clark and served as a major trading factory until
       1822 when it was abandoned.

286.   Griffis, Joseph K.   (Chief Tahan).   Tahan: Out of
       Savagery into Civilization.   New York: George H.
       Doran Company, 1915.

287.   Grove, Nettie Thompson.   "Fort Osage, First Settle-

ment in Jackson County" in Missouri Valley Historical Society Publications. Volume I. Kansas City,
Missouri, pp. 56-70.

In operation between 1808 and 1822, except for
an abandonment in 1813-1815, Fort Osage was an
important trading factory for the American government.

288. Hagan, William T. The Sac and Fox Indians. Norman:
University of Oklahoma Press, 1958. 284 pp.

Has many references to the Osages, who warred
upon the Sac and Fox habitually.

289. Hagan, William T. "The Sauk and Fox Treaty of 1804,"
Missouri Historical Review 51 (October 1956): 1-7.

290. Hampton, Carol. "Indian Colonization in the Cherokee
Outlet and Western Indian Territory," The Chronicles of Oklahoma 54 (Spring 1976): 130-145.

Contains information on the move of the Osages
from Kansas to Indian Territory.

291. Hargrett, Lester. A Bibliography of the Constitutions
and Laws of the American Indians. Cambridge:
Harvard University Press, 1947. 124 pp.

Among the printed documents relating to the internal government of 14 tribes are those of the
Osages. Included are descriptions of the 1861 and
1881 constitutions.

292. Harris, Frank H. "Neosho Agency 1838-1871," The
Chronicles of Oklahoma 43 (Spring 1965): 35-57.

The Osages, although distant from the agency,
were served by the agents stationed there while on
their Kansas reservation.

293. Henning, Dale R. "The Osage Nation: 1775-1818,"

in Osage Indians. New York: Garland Publishing,
Inc., 1974. Garland American Indian Ethnohistory
Series. Volume IV, pp. 295-325.

Henning's report as an expert witness before the
Indian Claims Commission attempted to demonstrate
exactly where the Osages lived in eastern Oklahoma
and northwestern Arkansas.

294. Hill, Edward E. Preliminary Inventory of the Records
of the Bureau of Indian Affairs. 2 vols. Washington, D.C.: National Archives and Records Service,
1965.

295. Hollon, W. Eugene. The Lost Pathfinder: Zebulon
Montgomery Pike. Norman: University of Oklahoma Press, 1949. 240 pp.

Includes the story of Pike's return of Osage cap-
tives to the tribe in 1806 and the explorer's visit
among the Osages.

296. Holman, Tom. "William G. Coffin, Lincoln's Super-
intendent of Indian Affairs for the Southern Super-
intendency," The Kansas Historical Quarterly 39
(Winter 1973): 491-514.

This well-researched article offers a good account of the Union's activities among the Kansas
tribes including the Osages.

297. Holway, Hope. "Union Mission, 1826-1837," The Chronicles of Oklahoma 40 (Winter 1962-1963): 355-378.

Tells more about the missionaries than their
Osage charges.

298. Houck, Louis. History of Missouri from the Earliest
Settlements Until the Admission of the State into
the Union. 3 vols. Chicago: R. R. Donnelley
and Sons, 1908.

The Osages are a major topic in this history that ends in 1820.

299. Houck, Louis, editor. Spanish Regime in Missouri. 2 vols. Chicago: R. R. Donnelley & Sons, 1909.

Contains papers and documents relating to Upper Louisiana taken from Spanish archives and translated into English. It is a major source for Osage/Spanish relations.

300. Howes, Charles C. This Place Called Kansas. Norman: University of Oklahoma Press, 1952. 236 pp.

301. Hoyt, George H. Kansas and the Osage Swindle. Washington, D. C. : Gibson Brothers, Printers, 1868.

This pamphlet castigated the proposed treaty between the U. S. and the Osages that would have awarded most of the tribe's Kansas reserve to railroad interests.

302. Huckaby, George Portal. "The Osage Indians and Their Treaty Relations with the Federal Government." MA thesis, Oklahoma A & M, 1936.

Not much analysis in this rather dry recital of treaty terms.

303. Hunter, John Dunn. Manners and Customs of Several Indian Tribes Located West of the Mississippi ... . Philadelphia: J. Maxwell, 1823. Reprinted by Ross and Haines, Minneapolis, Minnesota, 1957; the Johnson Reprint Corporation, New York, 1968; and Schocken Books, New York, 1973. Edited by Richard Drinnon.

Although its authenticity has been disputed, recent scholarship suggests that this narrative by a white captive of Indians, including the Osages, is an important and accurate firsthand account of tribal life in the 1790s and early 1800s.

304. "Indian Treaties and Councils Affecting Kansas," Trans-
      actions of the Kansas State Historical Society 16
      (1923-1925): 746-772.

           Lists all of the Osage treaties between 1806 and
      1870 with the general terms and signatories.

305. Isern, Thomas D., editor. "Exploration and Diplomacy:
      George Champlin Sibley's Report to William Clark,
      1811," Missouri Historical Review 73 (October 1978):
      85-102.

           Enhanced by several good illustrations, this edited
      version of Sibley's 1811 journey from Fort Osage
      onto the prairies contains a great deal of information
      on the Osages.

306. Isern, Thomas. "George Champlin Sibley, 1811 and
      1825-1826," in Joseph A. Stout, Jr., editor, Fron-
      tier Adventurers: American Exploration in Okla-
      homa. Oklahoma City: Oklahoma Historical So-
      ciety, 1976, pp. 19-37.

           Sibley, a U.S. government factor at Fort Osage
      in 1810, was guided by Osages on his 1811 expedi-
      tion into eastern Oklahoma and proceeded with tribal
      permission for his 1825-1826 travels.

307. Jackson, Donald, editor. The Journals of Zebulon
      Montgomery Pike with Letters and Related Docu-
      ments. 2 vols. Norman: University of Oklahoma
      Press, 1966.

           A valuable resource for the study of the Osages
      as Pike spent much time with them and was the
      official U.S. emissary dealing with the tribe.

308. Jackson, William Glenn. "Missions Among the Kick-
      apoo and Osage in Kansas, 1820-1860." MA thesis,
      Kansas State University, 1965.

309. Jahoda, Gloria. The Trail of Tears. New York: Holt,
      Rinehart and Winston, 1975. 356 pp.

In rather flowery prose this study concentrates
on the forced removal of the Five Civilized Tribes
to Arkansas and Oklahoma where some, especially
the Cherokees, came into conflict with the Osages,
who resented the intrusion.

310. Jayne, Mitchell F. Old Fishhawk. Philadelphia: J. B.
      Lippincott Company, 1970. 279 pp.

      The title character of this novel is an Osage who
      lives on the edge of white civilization.

311. John, Elizabeth A. H. Storms Brewed in Other Men's
      Worlds: The Confrontation of Indians, Spanish, and
      French in the Southwest, 1540-1795. College Sta-
      tion: Texas A & M University Press, 1975. 805
      pp.

      Although peripheral to the author's primary geo-
      graphic concern, the Osages are mentioned frequently
      in this excellent work which analyzes the tribe's
      interactions, mostly hostile, with other Indians.

312. Johnson, Steven L. Guide to American Indian Docu-
      ments in the Congressional Serial Set: 1817-1899.
      New York: Clearwater Publishing Co. , 1977. 503
      pp.

313. Jones, Charles Thomas, Jr. "George Champlin Sib-
      ley: The Prairie Puritan (1782-1863)." Ph. D. dis-
      sertation, University of Missouri, 1969.

      Sibley was the factor at Fort Osage beginning
      in 1810 and for many years after was very active
      in Osage affairs.

314. Kalloch, I. S. ; C. Robinson; A. N. Blackledge; and
      William Babcock. The Osage Treaty. n. p. , 1868.

      This pamphlet discusses the unratified treaty of
      1868 that would have given much of the Osages'
      Kansas lands to railroads. It is part of the Sidney

Clarke Papers held by the Osage Museum in Pawhuska, Oklahoma.

315. Keiser, Albert. The Indian in American Literature. New York: Octagon Books, 1970. 312 pp.

The Osages are discussed in terms of their depiction by Washington Irving and as nouveau riche oil Indians.

316. Keller, Robert H. , Jr. American Protestantism and United States Indian Policy, 1869-82. Lincoln: University of Nebraska Press, 1983. 359 pp.

The Osage tribe's first Quaker agent, Isaac Gibson, and some of his experiences in the early 1870s with the tribe are briefly chronicled.

317. Kinnaird, Lawrence. "American Penetration into Spanish Territory, 1776-1803. " Ph. D. dissertation, University of California, Berkeley, 1928.

The Osages were much concerned with the encroachment of the U. S. into the territory of their Spanish ally, and none too happy at the accomplished fact.

318. Kinnaird, Lawrence, editor. "Clark-Leyba Papers," American Historical Review 21 (October 1935): 92-112.

Captain Fernando de Leyba was commander of the Arkansas Post in the early 1770s and experienced considerable difficulty in dealing with the Osages.

319. Kinnaird, Lawrence, editor. Spain in the Mississippi Valley, 1763-1794. American Historical Association Annual Report for 1945. 3 parts in Volumes II, III, and IV. Washington, D. C. , 1949.

320. Kinney, J. P. A Continent Lost--A Civilization Won:

Indian Land Tenure in America. Baltimore: The
Johns Hopkins Press, 1937. 366 pp.

This general treatise includes some specific ex-
amples involving the Osages and their treaties.

321. Kvasnicka, Robert M. , and Herman J. Viola, editors.
The Commissioners of Indian Affairs, 1824-1977.
Lincoln: University of Nebraska Press, 1979. 384
pp.

Experts in the field of Indian history offer their
analyses of the Indian Commissioners. Some of
the articles refer specifically to the Osages.

322. Kyte, George W. "A Spy on the Western Waters: The
Military Intelligence Mission of General Collot in
1796," Mississippi Valley Historical Review 34 (December 1957): 427-442.

Collot, a Frenchman, visited the Osages on his
1796 journey.

323. Latrobe, Charles Joseph. The Rambler in Oklahoma:
Latrobe's Tour with Washington Irving. Edited by
Muriel H. Wright and George H. Shirk. Oklahoma
City: Harlow Publishing Company, 1955. 92 pp.

Latrobe accompanied the Washington Irving expedition of 1832 and included commentary on the
Osages in his letters, some of them reprinted from
his 1835 book.

324. Lawson, Lewis A. "Old Fish Hawk: From Stereotype
to Archetype," American Indian Quarterly 3 (Winter
1977-78): 321-333.

The character of Old Fish Hawk in the novel by
Mitchell F. Jayne is Osage.

325. Lewis, Anna. Along the Arkansas. Dallas, Texas:
The Southwest Press, 1932. 207 pp.

Two chapters describing the La Harpe and Du
Tisné expeditions between 1718 and 1722 contain
some description of the Osages.

326.   Lewis, Anna.   Chief Pushmataha, American Patriot:
The Story of the Choctaws' Struggle for Survival.
New York: Exposition Press, 1959.   204 pp.

Contains a good descriptive account of early con-
frontations between the Choctaws and Osages in the
early 1800s.

327.   Lewis, Anna.   "Du Tisné's Expedition into Oklahoma,
1719," The Chronicles of Oklahoma 3 (December
1925):   319-322.

Du Tisné was the first official representative
of the French government to visit the Osages.

328.   Lewis, Anna.   "La Harpe's First Expedition into Oklahoma, 1718-1719," The Chronicles of Oklahoma
2 (December 1924):   331-349.

La Harpe's expedition was frightened by Osage
hunting parties, which extorted gifts from the Frenchmen and their Caddoan guides.

329.   Lewis, Meriwether, and George Rogers Clark.   Journals.   Edited by Bernard De Voto.   Boston: Houghton Mifflin Company, 1953.

These famous explorers had only slight contact
with the Osages in 1804 during their expedition,
but their later careers were intertwined closely with
the tribe's affairs.

330.   Liljegren, Ernest R.   "The Commission of Carlos
Howard."   MA thesis, University of Southern California, 1936.

Lieutenant Colonel Charles Howard was sent by
the Louisiana Spanish government to reinforce de-

fenses against possible British attack and American
encroachment in Upper Louisiana near the Osages
in 1796.

331. Littlefield, Daniel F. , Jr. "Washington Irving and the
      American Indian," American Indian Quarterly 5 (May
      1979): 135-154.

      Comments on why Irving viewed the Osages as
      "the noblest Indians."

332. Loehr, Norbert P. "Federal Relations with the Jesuit
      Osage Indian Mission, 1847-1870." MA thesis, St.
      Louis University, 1940.

      The Jesuits were extremely influential among the
      Osages during this period on their Kansas reserve.

333. Loomis, Noel M. , and Abraham P. Nasatir. Pedro
      Vial and the Roads to Santa Fe. Norman: Univer-
      sity of Oklahoma Press, 1967. 569 pp.

      Includes an excellent and illuminating discussion
      of the Osages' activities as plains raiders, as far
      southwest as Santa Fe, in the 1780s and 1790s.

334. Marriott, Alice, and Carol K. Rachlin. American
      Epic: The Story of the American Indian. New
      York: G. P. Putnam's Sons, 1969. 254 pp.

      The Osages are the focus of the authors' discus-
      sion of Indian-Spanish-French relations in the
      seventeenth, eighteenth, and nineteenth centuries.

335. Martin, Lloydine. "George Victor Collot in the Mis-
      sissippi Valley." MA thesis, University of Cali-
      fornia, Berkeley, 1935.

      A French general, Collot traveled in Upper Louis-
      iana in 1798, presumed by the Spanish to be a spy
      as he met with Osages among other tribes in the
      region.

336.   Martin, Ramona I. "Government Treatment of the Os-
       ages to 1830."   MA thesis, Wichita University,
       1934.

          Mostly concentrates on the treaties forced upon
          the Osages in Missouri and Arkansas causing them
          to vacate their lands for a Kansas reservation.

337.   Mathews, John Joseph. The Osages: Children of the
       Middle Waters. Norman: University of Oklahoma
       Press, 1961. Paperback edition by University of
       Oklahoma Press, 1982.   823 pp.

          Written by a mixed-blood Osage, it contains a
          massive ethnohistorical account of the tribe from
          before white contact until 1920.   Presented in an
          almost ahistorical style, it contains invaluable in-
          sights gained from the author's personal interviews
          with tribal elders.

338.   Mayhall, Mildred P. The Kiowas. Norman: Univer-
       sity of Oklahoma Press, 1962.   315 pp.

          The Osages were constant enemies of the Kiowas
          until General M. Arbuckle brought the tribes to a
          permanent peace.

339.   McCleave, David H. "A History of the Indian Mission
       of the Presbyterian Church in Kansas." MA thesis,
       Hays State College (Kansas), 1935.

          The Union mission in Neosho County established
          for the Osages in the 1820s is the main topic of
          this thesis.

340.   McCoy, John C. "Survey of Kansas Indian Lands,"
       Transactions of the Kansas State Historical Society
       4 (1886-1888): 298-311.

          Interesting account of McCoy's 1836 surveying
          party's encounter with the Osages and of Major
          A. L. Langham's in the late 1820s.

341. McDermott, John Francis. "Isaac McCoy's Second Ex-
      ploring Trip in 1828," The Kansas Historical Quar-
      terly 8 (August 1945): 400-462.

          McCoy, a Baptist missionary, accompanied an
      expedition of eastern tribes in 1828, visiting the
      west looking for homes. His party stopped at sev-
      eral Osage villages on the tribe's Kansas reserva-
      tion.

342. McDermott, John Francis. "Pierre Laclède and the
      Chouteaus," Missouri Historical Society Bulletin 21
      (July 1965): 279-283.

          The Chouteaus were first introduced to the Osages
      by Laclède.

343. McDermott, John Francis. "The Exclusive Trade Priv-
      ilege of Maxent, Laclède and Company," Missouri
      Historical Review 29 (July 1935): 272-278.

          One of the most lucrative aspects of the monopoly
      was the trade with the Osages.

344. McDermott, John Francis, editor. The Spanish in the
      Mississippi Valley, 1762-1804. Urbana: University
      of Illinois Press, 1974. 421 pp.

          Contains a chapter by Carl H. Chapman on the
      Osages tribal life between 1763 and 1804, including
      a description of the political organization, mourning-
      war ceremony, and method of warfare.

345. McDermott, John Francis, editor. Tixier's Travels
      on the Osage Prairies. Trans. by Albert J. Sal-
      van. Norman: University of Oklahoma Press,
      309 pp.

          The Osages--villages, chiefs, life-style, cus-
      toms--are a main topic of Victor Tixier's trans-
      lated Voyage aux prairies osages. Tixier spent
      several months with the tribe in 1840 including ac-

companying them on their summer hunt, and his
descriptions are the basis of much of the later writings on the aboriginal Osage.

346.   McKenney, Thomas L. , and James Hall.   The Indian
       Tribes of North America with Biographical Sketches
       and Anecdotes of the Principal Chiefs.   3 vols.
       New edition edited by Frederick Webb Hodge and
       David I. Bushnell, Jr. Edinburgh: John Grant,
       1934.

       In volume two there is a brief article on Le Sol-
       dat du Chene (The Soldier of the Oak) with a superb
       color portrait in profile.

347.   McReynolds, Edwin C.   Missouri: A History of the
       Crossroads State.   Norman: University of Okla-
       homa Press, 1962.   483 pp.

348.   Mead, J. R.   "The Little Arkansas," Transactions of
       the Kansas State Historical Society 10 (1907-1908):
       7-14.

       Offers an eyewitness description of some Osage
       villages and leaders, Little Bear and Nopowalla.

349.   Mercier, Marcus de.   "Letonnante Fortune des Indiens
       Osages," Revue Mondial 191, 292-299.

350.   Meyer, Duane G.   The Heritage of Missouri.   Saint
       Louis, Missouri: River City Publishers Limited,
       1963.   836 pp.

351.   Miller, Nyle H. , editor.   "Surveying the Southern
       Boundary Line of Kansas: From the Private Jour-
       nal of Col. Joseph E. Johnston," The Kansas His-
       torical Quarterly 1 (February 1932):   104-139.

       Johnston's 1857 surveying party encountered Os-
       age bands on two occasions.

352. Miner, H. Craig. Wichita: The Early Years, 1865-
      80. Lincoln: University of Nebraska Press, 1982.
      201 pp.

      Contains a good account of the Osages being pres-
      sured to leave their Kansas reservation between
      1865 and 1870.

353. Miner, H. Craig, and William E. Unrau. The End of
      Indian Kansas: A Study of Cultural Revolution, 1854-
      1871. Lawrence: University of Kansas Press, 1978.

      The Osages were the last of the tribes in Kan-
      sas that were removed to give up their reservation.
      Has an excellent analysis of the politics of removal.

354. Moore, John Preston. "Antonio de Ulloa: Profile of
      the First Spanish Governor of Louisiana," Louisiana
      History 8 (Summer 1967): 189-219.

      Ulloa's haughty attitude, together with the im-
      perious nature of the Osages, got relations between
      the two powers off to a period of brinksmanship
      for two decades.

355. Morehouse, George P. "History of the Kansa or Kaw
      Indians," Transactions of the Kansas State Histori-
      cal Society 10 (1907-1908): 327-368.

      Accompanied by several good photographs, this
      account of the Kaw includes many references to the
      Osages who were their constant enemies until Ze-
      bulon Pike brought peace to them. Thereafter the
      tribes were closely allied.

356. Morley, Helen Lucile. "A Brief History of the Osage
      Indians." MA thesis, Ohio State University, 1930.

357. Morris, Wayne. "Auguste Pierre Chouteau, Merchant
      Prince at the Three Forks of the Arkansas," The
      Chronicles of Oklahoma 48 (Summer 1970): 155-163.

Chouteau's post at the junction of the Verdigris, Grand, and Arkansas rivers depended on good relations with the Osages who trapped and raided in that area.

358.   Morris, Wayne. "Traders and Factories on the Arkansas Frontier, 1805-1822," Arkansas Historical Quarterly 28 (Spring 1969): 28-48.

359.   Morrison, T. F. "Mission Neosho, the First Kansas Mission," Kansas Historical Quarterly 4 (1935): 227-234.

Good description of the United Foreign Missionary Society's activities among the Osages in the 1820s and 1830s.

360.   Morrison, T. F. "The Osage Treaty of 1865," Transactions of the Kansas State Historical Society 17 (1926-1928): 692-708.

The 1865 treaty witnessed the ceding of the entire eastern portion of the Kansas reservation and came as a result of exceptional pressure on the tribe.

361.   Murchison, Kenneth S. Digest of Decisions Relating to Indian Affairs. 2 vols. Washington, D. C.: Government Printing Office, 1901. Reprinted by Kraus Reprint Company, Millwood, New York, 1973.

Has an excellent selection of Osage material mostly concerned with land cessions and disputed treaties.

362.   Nasatir, Abraham P., editor. "An Account of Spanish Louisiana, 1785," Missouri Historical Review 24 (July 1930): 521-536.

363.   Nasatir, Abraham P. "Anglo-Spanish Rivalry on the Upper Missouri," Mississippi Valley Historical Re-

view 16 (December 1929): 359-382; (March 1930): 420-439.

The trade and friendship of the Osages was a major point of contention between the two colonial powers.

364.   Nasatir, Abraham P. , editor.   Before Lewis and Clark: Documents Illustrating the History of Missouri, 1785-1804.   2 vols.   St. Louis: St. Louis Historical Documents Foundation, 1952.   853 pp.

365.   Nasatir, Abraham P.   "Ducharmé's Invasion of Missouri," Missouri Historical Review 24 (October 1929):   3-25; (January 1930):   238-260; (April 1930):   420-439.

An excellent account of the 1773 secret invasion of Jean Marie Ducharmé, a Canadian trader from British Illinois, down the Missouri River to trade with the Little Osages and Missouris.

366.   Nasatir, Abraham P.   "Jacques Clamorgan: Colonial Promoter of the Northern Border of New Spain," New Mexico Historical Review 17 (April 1942): 101-112.

Clamorgan was the leader of the Upper Missouri Traders, who included the Osages among their customers and suppliers.

367.   Nasatir, Abraham P.   "The Anglo-Spanish Frontier in the Illinois Country During the American Revolution, 1779-1783," Journal of the Illinois State Historical Society 21 (October 1928):   291-358.

368.   Nasatir, Abraham P.   "The Chouteaus and the Indian Trade of the West, 1763-1852."   MA thesis, University of California, Berkeley, 1922.

The Chouteau brothers, Auguste and Pierre, played an extremely important role in Osage affairs in the 1790s and early 1800s.

369. Nasatir, Abraham P. "Trade and Diplomacy in the
     Spanish Illinois, 1763-1792." Ph. D. dissertation,
     University of California, Berkeley, 1926.

     Includes some aspects of Spanish policy toward
     the Osages.

370. Newman, Tillie Karns. The Black Dog Trail. Boston:
     Christopher Publishing House, 1957. Reissue in
     paper, 1976. 224 pp.

     A somewhat romantic, informal history of the
     Osages between 1800 and 1900 which contains some
     worthwhile quotations and references gleaned from
     oral and hard-to-find written and manuscript sour-
     ces.

371. Nichols, Roger L. The Missouri Expedition, 1818-
     1820. The Journal of Surgeon John Gale with Re-
     lated Documents. Norman: University of Oklahoma
     Press, 1969. 140 pp.

     Contains some scattered brief references to the
     Osages.

372. Nuttall, Thomas. A Journal of Travels into the Ar-
     kansas Territory During the Year 1819 with Occa-
     sional Observations on the Manners of the Aborig-
     ines. Philadelphia, 1821. New edition edited by
     Savoie Lottinville. Norman: University of Okla-
     homa Press, 1980. 389 pp.

     Nuttall, a botanist from England, made careful
     observations of the Osages in Arkansas recording
     details of a council at Fort Smith. His is among
     the most informative of the primary sources avail-
     able on the tribe.

373. O'Gallaghan, Mary A. M. "The Indian Policy of Car-
     ondelet in Spanish Louisiana, 1792-1797." Ph. D.
     dissertation, University of California, Berkeley,
     1941.

The Osages were among the most important tribes
under Spanish dominion during Carondelet's term as
governor.

374. Oglesby, Richard Edward. Manuel Lisa and the Opening of the Missouri Fur Trade. Norman: University of Oklahoma Press, 1963. 246 pp.

Based on extensive archival materials, this study
sheds much light on the fur-trading activities of the
Osages. Lisa was granted a monopoly on the Osage
trade in 1802.

375. Oswalt, Wendell H. This Land Was Theirs: A Study
of the North American Indian. New York: John
Wiley & Sons, Inc., 1966. 560 pp.

The Osages are discussed mostly in relation to
their wars with the Sauk and Fox tribes.

376. Owens, M. Lillianna. "The Guiding Light of the Osages," Catholic Educational Review 39 (September
1941): 414-420.

A brief discussion of the mission schools run
by the Jesuits in Kansas for Osage children and
especially the efforts of Father Schoenmakers.

377. Parks, Harry G. "Removal of Indians from Kansas."
MA thesis, Colorado State University, 1934.

378. Parsons, David. "The Removal of the Osages from
Kansas." Ph.D. dissertation, University of Oklahoma, 1940.

An exhaustively researched study, it has been
utilized by every scholar interested in the politics
of Osage removal from Kansas to Indian Territory
in 1871.

379. Peake, Ora Brooks. A History of the United States

Indian Factory System 1795-1822. Denver: Sage
Books, 1954. 340 pp.

Contains an account of the establishment of the
factory at Fort Osage in 1808 and its subsequent
history.

380.   Ponziglione, Paul N. "Osage Mission During the Civil
War," St. Louis Catholic Historical Review 4 (1922):
219-229.

The Jesuit-run mission was in the midst of the
war which saw Osages fighting on both sides and
Father Schoenmakers, an ardent Unionist, having
to flee his home at one point.

381.   Prucha, Francis Paul. A Bibliographical Guide to the
History of Indian-White Relations in the United States.
Chicago: University of Chicago Press, 1977. 454 pp.

382.   Prucha, Francis Paul. American Indian Policy in the
Formative Years: The Indian Trade and Intercourse
Acts, 1790-1834. Lincoln: University of Nebraska
Press, 1962. 303 pp.

The Osages figure in this fine study primarily
in regard to the 1808-1820 period having to do with
land cessions and trade agreements with the federal government.

383.   Prucha, Francis Paul. Indian Peace Medals in American History. Lincoln: University of Nebraska
Press, 1971. 186 pp.

Zebulon Pike's visit to the Osages is discussed
and there is a full page picture of Chief Pawhuska.

384.   Prucha, Francis Paul. Indian-White Relations in the
United States: A Bibliography of Works Published
1975-1980. Lincoln: University of Nebraska Press,
1982. 179 pp.

385. Redwine, Baird Albian. "Indian Relations in Arkansas."
      MA thesis, University of Colorado, 1931.

      The Claremore band of Osages was located in
      Arkansas in the first three decades of the nine-
      teenth century.

386. Riley, Franklin L. "Spanish Policy in Missouri After
      the Treaty of San Lorenzo" in American Historical
      Association Annual Report, 1897. Washington, D.C.,
      1898, pp. 177-191.

387. Robertson, James Alexander, editor. Louisiana Under
      the Rule of Spain, France, and the United States,
      1785-1807. 2 vols. Cleveland: The Arthur H.
      Clark Co., 1911.

      Contains contemporary accounts of Louisiana,
      including Osage territory, from French, Spanish,
      English, and American officials.

388. Rollings, Willard H. "Prairie Hegemony: An Ethno-
      historical Study of the Osage from Early Times to
      1840." Ph.D. dissertation, Texas Tech University,
      1893.

      This massive ethnohistory is exceptionally well-
      researched and is an excellent source for early
      Osage culture and history.

389. Rowse, Edward Francis. "Auguste and Pierre Chou-
      teau." Ph.D. dissertation, Washington University,
      1936.

      The Chouteaus were very active in Osage affairs
      from the 1790s to the early 1800s as traders and
      diplomats.

390. Royce, Charles C., editor. "Indian Land Cessions
      in the United States," in Bureau of American Eth-
      nology Eighteenth Annual Report, 1896-1897. Vol-
      ume 2. Washington, D.C., 1897.

391. Russell, Jason Almus. "Irving: Recorder of Indian
      Life," The Journal of American History 25 (1931):
      185-195.

          Irving encountered Osages among other Indians
          on his travels on the plains.

392. Ryan, Harold W. , editor. "Jacob Bright's Journal of
      a Trip to the Osage Indians," The Journal of South-
      ern History 15 (November 1949): 509-523.

          Reproduces several letters written by Bright, an
          Indian trader, in 1806, describing the Arkansas
          band of Osages under Chief Claremore (Clermont).

393. Sampson, Francis A. "Glimpses of Old Missouri by
      Explorers and Travelers," Missouri Historical Re-
      view 1 (July 1907): 247-266.

          Virtually all of the explorers and travelers men-
          tioned visited the Osages and many of their descrip-
          tions are included in the article.

394. Schmeckebier, Laurence F.   The Office of Indian Af-
      fairs: Its History, Activities and Organization.
      Baltimore: The Johns Hopkins Press, 1927.   591
      pp.

          The author offers a brief history of the Osage
          tribe's relations with the U. S. with a lengthy quota-
          tion from an Indian inspector on the effect of oil
          wealth on the people.

395. Schoolcraft, Henry Rowe.   Historical and Statistical
      Information Respecting the History, Conditions and
      Prospects of the Indian Tribes of the United States.
      6 vols.   Philadelphia: Lippincott, Grambo & Com-
      pany, 1851-1857.

396. Schoolcraft, Henry Rowe.   Scenes and Adventures in
      the Semi-Alpine Region of the Ozark Mountains in
      Missouri and Arkansas.   Philadelphia: Lippincott,
      Grambo & Company, 1853.

397.   Shea, John Gilmary.   History of the Catholic Missions
       Among the Indian Tribes of the United States, 1529-
       1854.   New York: Edward Dunigan & Brother, 1855.
       514 pp.

            Includes an account of the La Croix and Van
            Quickenborne Osage mission activities and provides
            the "Our Father" prayer in Osage.

398.   Shoemaker, Floyd C.   Early History of Halley's Bluff,
       Osage Indian Villages and Harmony Mission.   Ne-
       vada, Mo. , n. d.

399.   Short, Emma Jean.   "The Culture of the Osage Indians
       in Missouri."   MA thesis, University of Missouri,
       1934.

400.   Sibley, Major George C.   "Extracts from Diary," The
       Chronicles of Oklahoma 5 (June 1927):   196-218.

            Offers an account of Sibley's 1811 expedition
            leaving from Fort Osage and accompanied by a
            dozen Osages.

401.   Sibley, George C.   "Indian Mode of Life in Missouri
       and Kansas," Missouri Historical Review 9 (October
       1914):   43-50.

            Reprints 1820 letters of George Sibley, the factor
            at Fort Osage, to Thomas McKenney, Superintend-
            ent of Indian trade, describing the Arkansas band
            of Osages.

402.   Sibley, John.   "Historical Sketches of the Several In-
       dian Tribes in Louisiana... ," Annals of Congress,
       9th Cong. , 2d sess. , Appendix, pp. 1075-1087.

403.   Simmons, Eva Mary.   "Cherokee-Osage Relations:
       1803-1839."   MA thesis, University of Oklahoma,
       1940.

During a good part of this period the two tribes were fierce enemies engaged in continuous raiding and warfare.

404. Smallwood, James. "Major Stephen Harriman Long, 1820," in Joseph A. Stout, Jr. , editor, Frontier Adventurers: American Exploration in Oklahoma. Oklahoma City: Oklahoma Historical Society, 1976, pp. 51-60.

The Long expedition found Osages on a largely futile expedition, and members of the party kept copious notes of their observations of tribal life.

405. Smith, Ralph A. "Account of the Journey of Bénard de la Harpe: Discovery Made by Him of Several Nations Situated in the West," Southwestern Historical Quarterly 62 (July 1958-April 1959): 73-86, 246-259, 371-385, 525-541.

La Harpe was among the first Frenchmen to come into contact with the Osages.

406. Smith, Ralph A. "Exploration of the Arkansas River by Bénard de la Harpe, 1721-1722," Arkansas Historical Quarterly 10 (Fall 1951): 339-363.

La Harpe visited the Osages among others.

407. Spaulding, George F. , editor. On the Western Tour with Washington Irving: The Journal and Letters of Count de Pourtalès. Norman: University of Oklahoma Press, 1968. 96 pp.

Pourtalès mentions the Osages throughout his journal and letters.

408. Skaggs, Jimmy M. "Captain Nathan Boone, 1843," in Joseph A. Stout, Jr. , editor, Frontier Adventurers: American Exploration in Oklahoma. Oklahoma City: Oklahoma Historical Society, 1976, pp. 111-123.

Daniel Boone's son Nathan was one of the Mis-
sourians who contributed to the harassment of the
Osages from that state in 1808, but in 1843 he used
them as guides in locating the salt licks in northeastern Oklahoma.

409.   Steffen, Jerome O.   William Clark: Jeffersonian Man
       on the Frontier.   Norman: University of Oklahoma
       Press, 1977.   196 pp.

       Includes an interesting analysis of Clark's nego-
       tiations with the Osages that resulted in the tribe's
       cession of two-thirds of present Missouri and one-
       half of present Arkansas.

410.   Stipes, M. F.   "Fort Orleans, the First French Post
       on the Missouri," Missouri Historical Review 8
       (April 1914):   121-135.

       Founded in 1723, the fort was a major base for
       French trading and political activities among the
       Osages.

411.   Stout, Joseph A. , Jr. , editor.   Frontier Adventurers:
       American Exploration in Oklahoma.   Oklahoma City:
       Oklahoma Historical Society, 1976.   158 pp.

       Contains several articles on such explorers as
       Sibley, Nuttall, and Long, who encountered the Os-
       ages on their travels.

412.   Sutton, Imre.   Indian Land Tenure: Bibliographical
       Essays and a Guide to the Literature.   New York:
       Clearwater Publishing Co. , 1975.   290 pp.

       Includes a discussion of the works of three writ-
       ers who have dealt with Osage land.

413.   Terrell, John Upton.   Land Grab: The Truth About
       "The Winning of the West."   New York: The Dial
       Press, 1972.   277 pp.

There is an entire chapter devoted to the removal of the Osages from their Kansas reserve to
the tribe's last reservation in Oklahoma.

414.   Thomas, Clarence Lot, editor.   Annotated Acts of Con-
       gress: Five Civilized Tribes and the Osage Nation.
       Columbia, Mo.: E. W. Stephens Publishing Com-
       pany, 1913.   347 pp.

       A very useful compendium that includes many
       of the acts of Congress pertaining to and uniquely
       affecting the Osages.

415.   Thomas, James. "The Osage Removal to Oklahoma,"
       The Chronicles of Oklahoma 55 (Spring 1977): 46-
       55.

       Based on published government documents, this
       brief, superficial article outlines the events taking
       place on and around the Osage reservation in Kan-
       sas between 1858 and 1871 that led to the tribe's
       reluctant removal to Oklahoma.

416.   Thomas, John L. "Some Historic Lines in Missouri,"
       Missouri Historical Review 3 (January 1909): 210-
       233.

       Discusses the 1808 Osage treaty and the result-
       ing surveys to establish the tribe's territorial limits.

417.   Thomas, Marjorie Oletha. "The Arkansas Post of
       Louisiana, 1682-1783." MA thesis, University of
       California, Berkeley, 1948.

       The post was located near the Osage villages.

418.   Thomas, Phillip Drennon. "Thomas James, Hugh Glenn,
       and Jacob Fowler, 1821-1823," in Joseph A. Stout,
       Jr. , editor, Frontier Adventurers: American Ex-
       ploration in Oklahoma. Oklahoma City: Oklahoma
       Historical Society, 1976, pp. 61-79.

Fowler was active in Osage-Cherokee affairs and his journal contains some interesting observations about the tribe.

419. Thompson, Paul. "Cherokee and Osage Met in Battle Near Claremore in 1818," The American (Tulsa, Oklahoma) 3 (1929): 12.

420. Thwaites, Reuben Gold, editor. Jesuit Relations and Allied Documents. 73 vols. Cleveland: Arthur H. Clark Company, 1896-1901.

This is an exceptionally important primary source for Osage history as the Jesuits maintained missions among the Osages and were very influential in tribal affairs.

421. Timouran, A. "Catholic Exploration of the Far West, 1794-1835," Records of the American Catholic Historical Society 48 (1937): 329-387; 49 (1938): 50-66, 135-170.

Includes quite a lot on explorers who visited Osages.

422. Tracy, Joseph. History of American Missions to the Heathen, from Their Commencement to the Present Time. Worcester, Mass.: Spooner & Howland, 1840. 726 pp. Reprinted by Johnson Reprint Corporation, New York, 1970.

Includes the activities of the American Board of Commissioners for Foreign Missions among the Osages.

423. Tracy, Valerie. "The Indian in Transition: The Neosho Agency 1850-1861," The Chronicles of Oklahoma 48 (Summer 1970): 164-183.

A well-researched study of the agency which served the Osages and several other tribes.

424.   Trenfels (Treatafeles), Jacqueline T. "Spanish Occupa-
        tion of the Upper Mississippi Valley, 1765-1770."
        MA thesis, University of California, Berkeley, 1941.

        The Osages were located in the area and their
        strategic position along the major river system
        made them an important object of Spanish policy.

425.   Tuttle, Sarah. Osage Missions. Boston: Sabbath
        School Union, 1831.

        Letters from Cornelia Pelham to her family con-
        cerning the Chickasaw and Osage mission stations.

426.   Tyler, S. Lyman. A History of Indian Policy. Wash-
        ington, D. C. : United States Department of the In-
        terior, Bureau of Indian Affairs, 1973.   328 pp.

427.   United States Department of War. The War of Rebel-
        lion: A Compilation of the Union and Confederate
        Armies.   4 series.   70 vols.   128 books.   Washing-
        ton, D. C. : Government Printing Office, 1880-1901.

        The Osages fought on both sides during the Civil
        War and their Kansas reservation was invaded by
        federal troops.

428.   Unrau, William E.   The Kansas Indians: A History of
        the Wind People, 1673-1873.   Norman: University
        of Oklahoma Press, 1971.

        The Kansas, later called the Kaw, are related
        to the Osages and were removed to Indian Terri-
        tory at the same time, sharing the Osage reserve
        there.

429.   Vaill, William F. "Annual Report," Missionary Herald
        29 (1833): 369.

        One of his fellow missionaries died and Vaill re-
        ported that no church or school had been organized
        at Hopefield, an offshoot of Union and Harmony Mis-
        sions.

430. Vaill, William F. "Osage Indians," Missionary Herald
      22 (1826): 267-271.

      Vaill headed the ill-fated Hopefield Mission on
      the Neosho River that was to serve as an example
      of the white man's agricultural life.

431. Vaill, William F. "Osage Indians," Missionary Herald
      23 (1827): 146-148.

      Floods and sickness spoiled Vaill's efforts to con-
      vert the Osages to an agricultural life-style.

432. Villiers du Terrage, Marc de. "A Hitherto Unpublished
      Map of Fort Orleans on the Missouri," Mid-America
      12 (January 1930): 260-264.

      Contains information on the Osages near whose
      villages the fort was built in 1723.

433. Viola, Herman J. Thomas L. McKenney: Architect
      of America's Early Indian Policy: 1816-1830. Chi-
      cago: The Swallow Press, Inc., 1974. 365 pp.

      This biography of McKenney emphasizes his role
      as head of the early versions of the Indian Office.
      The Osages figured prominently in the period be-
      tween 1816-1830 in trade and removal matters.

434. Violette, Eugene Morrow. A History of Missouri.
      Boston: D. C. Heath & Co., Publishers, 1918. 500 pp.

435. Vissier, Paul. Histoire de la tribe des Osages. Paris:
      C. Béchet Libraire, 1827. 92 pp.

      An interesting account of the six Osages brought to
      France in the early 1820s for a visit.

436. Voget, Fred W. Osage Research Report in Osage In-
      dians. New York: Garland Publishing Company,
      Inc., 1974. Garland American Indian Ethnohistory
      Series. Volume I. 371 pp.

Compiled from primary sources, this account offers an ethnohistorical narrative of the Osages from the seventeenth century through 1825.

437. Wardell, Morris L. "Protestant Missions Among the Osages," The Chronicles of Oklahoma 2 (September 1924): 285-297.

A well-written narrative of the Union Mission to the Osages begun in 1820, and later the Harmony Mission in 1824; both activities closed in 1834.

438. Washburn, Wilcomb E. The American Indian and the United States: A Documentary History. 4 vols. New York: Random House, 1973.

In addition to the reports of the Indian Commissioners up to 1963, some of which refer specifically to Osage affairs, this document collection also includes the texts of two Osage treaties in 1808 and 1825.

439. Wedel, Mildred Mott. "Claude-Charles Du Tisné: A Review of His 1719 Journeys" Great Plains Journal 12 (Fall 1972): 5-25; (Spring 1973): 147-173.

Du Tisné's visit to the Osages was the first official one by the French.

440. Wedel, Mildred Mott. "J. B. Bénard, Sieur de la Harpe: Visitor to the Wichitas in 1719," Great Plains Journal 10 (Spring 1971): 37-70.

La Harpe encountered the Osage on this trip.

441. Wedel, Mildred Mott. "The Bénard de La Harpe Historiography on French Colonial Louisiana," Louisiana Studies 13 (Spring 1974): 9-67.

An exceptionally thorough listing of La Harpe's correspondence and writings. He provided one of the earliest descriptions of the Osages in 1719.

442. Wendels, Marie Anne. "French Interest in and Activities on the Spanish Border of Louisiana, 1717-1753."

MA thesis, University of California, Berkeley, 1914.

Mentions the Osages several times.

443. Westbrook, Harriette Johnson. "The Chouteaus: Their
      Contributions to the History of the West," The
      Chronicles of Oklahoma 11 (June-September 1933):
      786-797, 942-966.

      The Chouteaus were traders and representatives
      of the French and American governments to the Os-
      ages and extremely influential in tribal affairs.

444. Whitaker, Arthur Preston. "Antonio de Ulloa," His-
      panic American Historical Review 15 (May 1935):
      155-194.

      Ulloa's disdainful posture and Osage pride made his
      term as governor of Louisiana uneasy.

445. Whitaker, Arthur Preston. The Spanish American
      Frontier, 1783-1795. Boston: Houghton Mifflin
      Company, 1927. 255 pp.

446. White, Henry Ford. "The Economic and Social De-
      velopment of the Arkansas Prior to 1836." Ph. D.
      dissertation, University of Texas, 1931.

      Part of the Osages lived along the Arkansas
      River during this period.

447. Whitney, Henry C. The Osage Treaty. n. d. , n. p.

      This pamphlet discusses the unratified 1868 treaty
      between the U. S. and Osages. It can be found in
      the Sidney Clarke Papers held by the Osage Museum
      in Pawhuska, Oklahoma.

448. Wilhelm, Paul, Duke of Wurttemberg. Travels in North
      America, 1822-1824. Translated by W. Robert
      Nitske and edited by Savoie Lottinville. Norman:
      University of Oklahoma Press, 1973. 456 pp.

Offers some lengthy descriptions of the Osages
and their customs, including a fondness for alcohol.

449. Williams, Robert L. "Founding of the First Chouteau
      Trading Post in Oklahoma at Salina, Mayes County,"
      The Chronicles of Oklahoma 24 (Winter 1946-1947):
      483-491.

      Placed within the "Notes and Documents" section
      of the Chronicles, this report includes letters from
      several historians about whether John Pierre Chou-
      teau started a trading post in Oklahoma in addition
      to the family's Osage dealings.

450. Wilson, Terry P. "Claremore, the Osage, and the
      Intrusion of Other Indians, 1800-1824," in H. Glenn
      Jordan and Thomas M. Holm, editors, Indian Lead-
      ers: Oklahoma's First Statesmen. Oklahoma City:
      Oklahoma Historical Society, 1979, pp. 141-157.

      Deals with the internal politics of the Osages
      during a period of crisis with the Cherokees and
      other tribes.

451. Workers of the Writers' Program of the Works Prog-
      ress Administration in the State of Missouri, com-
      pilers. Missouri: A Guide to the "Show Me" State.
      New York: Duell, Sloan and Pearce, 1941. 652
      pp.

      A surprisingly thorough historical sketch of the
      Osages is included.

452. Zornow, William F. Kansas: A History of the Jay-
      hawk State. Norman: University of Oklahoma
      Press, 1957. 417 pp.

      The Osages figure in this state history mostly
      in their connection with early explorers and in the
      1860s, when Indian land titles were being extin-
      guished.

453. "Aged John Stink, Martyr, Expelled from Osage So-
     ciety," The American Indian (Tulsa, Oklahoma) 1
     (1926): 6.

     Another notice, apocryphal, about the tribe re-
     jecting John Stink, Ho-tah-moie, from its midst
     due to his having "returned from the dead" after
     being buried while in a comatose state.

454. Allen, C. M. The Sequoyah Movement. Oklahoma
     City: The Harlow Publishing Company, 1925.

     The Osages had two delegates at the Sequoyah
     convention that considered dual statehood for Okla-
     homa and Indian Territories.

455. "American Aristocracy," World's Work 34 (June 1917):
     139-140.

     A brief comment on the Osages and their oil
     wealth.

456. "American as Wampum," Time 57 (February 26, 1951):
     76-77.

     Deals with Maria Tallchief, the mixed-blood Os-
     age ballerina.

457. Anderson, Edward F. Peyote, The Divine Cactus.
     Tucson: University of Arizona Press, 1980.
     246 pp.

An excellent study of peyote, the hallucinogen
that was used as the sacrament for the cult, introduced to the Osages in the 1890s.   Contains some
specific references to the tribe's use of peyote.

458.   Anderson, Ken.   "Frank Frantz, Governor of Oklahoma
        Territory, 1906-1907," in Leroy H. Fischer, editor,
        Territorial Governors of Oklahoma.   Oklahoma City:
        Oklahoma Historical Society, 1975, pp. 128-144.

        Frantz, a former Rough Rider, was agent for
        the Osages just prior to being appointed territorial
        governor by Theodore Roosevelt.   His term in of-
        fice was troubled by accusations of corruption stem-
        ming from his days at the Osage Agency.

459.   "Apology for Murder," Independent 116 (February 20,
        1926):   227-228.

        Concerns the murder plot to kill Osages for their
        headright money.

460.   Bailey, Garrick Alan.   Changes in Osage Social Or-
        ganization, 1673-1906.   University of Oregon An-
        thropological Papers, No. 5.   Eugene, Oregon,
        1973.   122 pp.

        One of the most valuable works on the tribe
        based on field research and government documents.

461.   Bailey, Garrick Alan.   "Changes in Osage Social Or-
        ganization, 1673-1969."   Ph. D. dissertation, Uni-
        versity of Oregon, 1970.

        Emphasizes the effects of white contacts on Os-
        age custom leading to the disappearance of a care-
        fully balanced social system.

462.   Bailey, Garrick Alan.   "John Joseph Mathews" in Amer-
        ican Indian Intellectuals.   Proceedings of the Amer-
        ican Ethnological Society edited by Margot Liberty.
        New York: West Publishing Company, 1978.

A brief sketch of Mathews, the mixed-blood Osage Oxford graduate, who wrote several books fea-
turing his tribe and its reservation.

463. Bailey, Garrick Alan. "The Osage Roll: An Analysis,"
      The Indian Historian 5 (Spring 1972): 26-29.

      A comment on the fraud and resulting disposses-
      sion of the true Osages due to irregularities in the
      making of the 1908 tribal roll. Bailey testified in
      great detail before a Senate committee on this mat-
      ter.

464. Baird, W. David. The Osage People. Phoenix: In-
      dian Tribal Series, 1972. 104 pp.

      A very readable historical survey of the Osages
      enhanced by several excellent photographs, some in
      color.

465. Baldwin, George D. "Employment and Training Pat-
      terns of Native Americans on the Osage Reserva-
      tion." MA thesis, Oklahoma State University, 1978.

      Deals with the entire Indian population in Osage
      County, Osage and others, who are clients of the
      agency or seeking employment and training. This
      is more statistical than analytical.

466. Barney, Ralph A. Laws Relating to the Osage Tribe
      of Indians. Pawhuska, Okla. : The Osage Printery,
      Publishers, 1929.

      Contains every piece of federal legislation per-
      taining to the Osages. Copies available from the
      Osage Superintendency have more recent laws stapled
      to the back cover.

467. Beaver, R. Pierce. The Native American Christian
      Community: A Directory of Indian, Aleut, and Es-
      kimo Churches. Monrovia, Cal. : MARC, 1979.
      395 pp.

468.   Beckwith, H. T.   "Oil and Gas in Oklahoma," Okla-
        homa Geological Survey Bulletin, No. 40-T, 1928.

469.   "Black Curse of the Osages," Literary Digest 89 (April
        3, 1926):   42-44.

            Deals with the exploitation and violence visited
        upon the Osages as a result of their oil wealth.

470.   Bollinger, C. J.   "The Eastern Boundary of the Great
        Plains in North Central Oklahoma," Proceedings of
        the Oklahoma Academy of Science 5 (1925):   123-
        124.

            Description of the cross-timber line that bisects
        Osage County.

471.   "Book-of-the-Month," The Sooner Magazine 5 (Decem-
        ber 1932):   77, 90, 92.

            Gives the background of the choice of Osage John
        Joseph Mathews's Wah'Kon-Tah as the first Book-
        of-the-Month Club selection from a university press.
        Includes some information on the author's personal
        life and work habits.

472.   Boroff, D.   "Interview with Marjorie Tallchief and
        George Skibine," Dance Magazine 30 (December
        1956):   14-17.

            Marjorie and her sister Maria were mixed-blood
        Osage ballerinas.

473.   Bourlier, Bobby G.; Joe D. Nichols; William J. Ring-
        wald; P. J. Workman; and Stanley Clemmons.
        Soil Survey of Osage County, Oklahoma.   Washing-
        ton, D. C.:   National Cooperative Soil Survey, United
        States Department of Agriculture, 1979.

474.   Boutwell, Ruth.   "Adjustment of Osage Indian Youth
        to Contemporary Civilization."   MSW thesis, Uni-
        versity of Oklahoma, 1936.

Based on field work, this thesis includes a good
discussion of the effects of liquor and drugs on
Osage youth and the lingering instances of arranged
tribal marriages.

475. "Brilliant Bird: Firebird," Newsweek 34 (December
19, 1949): 75.

Describes the success of mixed-blood Osage ballerina Maria Tallchief.

476. Broad, William J. "The Osage Oil Cover-up," Science
208 (April 4, 1980): 32-35.

A short but well-written comment on the contro-
versy between the Army Corps of Engineers and
the Osages over plans to inundate valuable oil fields
with a man-made lake.

477. Brown, E. A. "Our Plutocratic Osage Indians,"
Travel 39 (October 1922): 19-22.

Includes some photographs of the Osages.

478. Burbank, E. A., and E. Royce. Burbank Among the
Indians. Caldwell, Idaho: The Caxton Printers,
1944. 232 pp.

Three or four pages are devoted to the Osages
at the height of their oil wealth.

479. Burchardt, Bill. "Osage Oil," The Chronicles of
Oklahoma 41 (Autumn 1963): 253-269.

Focuses primarily on the more dramatic aspects
of the impact of oil on the Osages in the 1920s;
decidedly an apologist for the surrounding Anglo-
American community's responsibility in the tribe's
financial exploitation.

480. Burgess, Larry E., and Lawrence M. Hauptman. The

Lake Mohonk Conference of Friends of the Indian: Guide to the Annual Reports. New York: Clearwater Publishing Co. , 1975. 164 pp.

481. Burns, Louis F. The Osage Annuity Rolls of 1878. 3 vols. Privately printed, 1980.

Lists the membership of the 14 existing bands of the tribe in 1873.

482. Burns, Louis F. Turn of the Wheel. Privately published by Louis F. Burns, 1980.

Available from the author who lives in Fallbrook, California, this is primarily a genealogy of the Burns and Tinker families of the Osage tribe with information on the Revards, Lesserts, and Roys as well.

483. Burrill, Robert Meredith. "Grasslands Empires: The Geography of Ranching in Osage County, Oklahoma, 1872-1965." Ph. D. dissertation, University of Kansas, 1970.

This well-researched study shows how most of the Osage allotments were alienated and many became parts of large ranching operations.

484. Burrill, Robert M[eredith]. "The Establishment of Ranching on the Osage Reservation," Geographical Review 62 (1972): 524-543.

Taken from his dissertation research, this piece documents the ways in which the rich grasslands of the Osage reserve were used by Kansas and Texas cattlemen through leasing arrangements and later by purchase of allotments.

485. Burrill, Robert M[eredith]. "The Osage Pasture Map," The Chronicles of Oklahoma 53 (Summer 1975): 204-211.

An excellent short study of the regularizing of
pasture leasing on the Osage reservation in the late
1890s.

486. Burwell, Kate P. "Richest People in the World,"
      Sturm's Oklahoma Magazine 2 (December 1924):
      89-93.

      A journalistic account of the tribe during the oil
      boom years that concentrates on the more spectacu-
      lar spending excesses of some Osage individuals.

487. "Bypaths of Kansas History," The Kansas Historical
      Quarterly 9 (August 1940): 312-323.

      Included in this collection of newspaper articles
      is one describing a 1901 Osage wedding in Oklahoma.

488. Callahan, Alice Anne. "The I'N-Lon Schka (Playground-
      of-the Eldest-Son); The June Ceremonial Dance of
      the Osages: A Study in American Indian Arts."
      Ph. D. dissertation, Syracuse University, 1977.

      A much broader study than the title implies,
      this excellent study includes a wealth of information
      on modern Osage ceremony and custom based on
      extensive field study.

489. Carpenter, C. C. Grand Rush for the Indian Territory.
      Independence, Kan. : P. H. Tiernan, 1879.

490. Carter, Clarence E. , editor. Territorial Papers of
      the United States. 26 vols. Washington, D. C. :
      Government Printing Office, 1934-1962.

491. Carter, James A. "Geology of the Pearsonia Area,
      Osage County, Oklahoma." Unpublished master's
      thesis, University of Oklahoma, 1954.

492. Carter, Kent, compiler. "Preliminary Inventory of the

Records of the Osage Indian Agency," 1974. Available at the regional branch of the National Archives located in the Federal Records Center at Fort Worth, Texas.

Not an official publication, the inventory describes the Osage tribal records comprising over 1,700 cubic feet of materials.

493. Cash, Joseph H. The Ponca People. Phoenix: Indian Tribal Series, 1975.

The Poncas not only live in close geographical proximity to the Osages but are frequent visitors at dances, having contributed many songs to the Osage tribal ceremonies.

494. Chapman, Berlin B. "Charles Curtis and the Kaw Reservation," The Kansas Historical Quarterly 14 (November 1947): 337-352.

The Kaw reservation was carved out of Osage land and the two tribes shared a single agent in Indian Territory after 1873.

495. Chapman, Berlin B. "Dissolution of the Osage," The Chronicles of Oklahoma 20 (September and December 1942): 244-254, 375-386; 21 (March and June 1943): 78-87, 171-182.

This four-part article details with great accuracy the politics and mechanics of the allotment of the reserve in 1906.

496. Cheadle, John Bogg, and T. G. Logan. Cases on Alienation and Descent of Indian Lands of the Five Civilized Tribes and the Osage Nation. Typescript, Copyright 1923.

Available at the Phillips Collection of Western History, University of Oklahoma, this study deals with individual members of the tribes and their allotments after severalty.

497.   Churchill, W. G. "Dance of Triumph: Braves Come
       Home from Battle Beyond the Seas and Their Tribes
       Celebrate," Collier's (June 29, 1946): 22-23.

       The Osages were one of the Indian tribes de-
       scribed in this illustrated article about returning
       World War II veterans.

498.   Clark, Ira G. "The Railroads and the Tribal Lands:
       Indian Territory, 1838-1890." Ph. D. dissertation,
       University of California, Berkeley, 1947.

499.   "Close Friend of Aged John Stink Gives Authentic Story
       on His Life," The American Indian (February 1927):
       4, 6.

       Attempts to dispel the myths surrounding John
       Stink (Ho-tah-moie), a full-blood Osage, through
       an interview with his guardian, but the myths are
       actually replaced with others.

500.   Cohen, Felix S. Handbook of Federal Indian Law.
       Washington, D. C.: Government Printing Office,
       1942.

       An especially valuable historical source about
       the Osages because of the many laws passed re-
       lating solely to that tribe.

501.   Collings, Ellsworth, and Alma Miller England. The
       101 Ranch. Norman: University of Oklahoma Press,
       1937. 249 pp.

       The 101 Ranch bordered the Osage reservation
       and shared much of the tribe's notoriety regarding
       oil wealth.

502.   Condra, G. E. "Opening of the Indian Territory,"
       American Geographic Society, Bulletin 39 (1907):
       1-20.

       Includes the politics behind the dissolution of the
       Osage and other Indian reservations prior to statehood.

503.   Cox, James.   Historical and Biographical Record of
        the Cattle Industry and the Cattlemen of Texas and
        Adjacent Territory.   St. Louis: Woodward and
        Tiernan Printing Co. , 1895.

            Contains some references to the use of the Osage
            reservation for grazing purposes by Kansas and
            Texas cattlemen.

504.   Cracraft, Marion.   "The Fabulous Osage," The Land-
        man (September 1967):   6-13; (October 1967):   24-
        29; (November 1967):   48-53.

            This three-part article concentrates on the de-
            velopment of the oil fields of the reservation.   It
            includes much technical information of a geological
            and drilling nature.

505.   Crowle, Pigeon.   "Maria Tallchief: Her Early Years,"
        Dance Magazine 30 (February 1956):   8+.

            This is an excerpt from Crowle's book Enter the
            Ballerina, which describes Tallchief, a mixed-blood
            Osage, during her childhood and youth.

506.   Dale, Edward Everett.   Oklahoma: The Story of a
        State.   Evanston, Ill. :   Row, Peterson and Com-
        pany, 1949.   448 pp.

            Very strong in its treatment of Indian topics,
            there are sections on various aspects of Osage
            history.

507.   Dale, Edward Everett.   "The Cherokee Strip Live Stock
        Association," The Chronicles of Oklahoma 5 (March
        1927):   58-78.

            Has a description of the Osages being removed
            from Kansas to Indian Territory and a good discus-
            sion of the cattle industry's use of their reserva-
            tion.

508. Davis, Clyde Brion. The Arkansas. New York: Far-
      rar & Rinehart, Inc. , 1940. 340 pp.

          Contains a brief description of the Osages' oil
      bonanza.

509. De Berry, Drue Lemuel. "The Ethos of the Oklahoma
      Oil Boom Frontier." MA thesis, University of Ok-
      lahoma, 1970.

          Concentrates on the excitement of the oil lease
      auctions and oil business during the period from
      1915 to 1930.

510. Debo, Angie. A History of the Indians of the United
      States. Norman: University of Oklahoma Press,
      1970. 464 pp.

          This comprehensive history of the American In-
      dian concentrates most heavily on the Native Amer-
      icans of Oklahoma and contains good coverage of
      the Osages.

511. Debo, Angie. Oklahoma: Foot-loose and Fancy-free.
      Norman: University of Oklahoma Press, 1949.

512. Debo, Angie. Tulsa: From Creek Town to Oil Capital.
      Norman: University of Oklahoma Press, 1943.
      123 pp.

          The Osages appear as characters in early Tulsa
      beginnings and later in the 1920s because the com-
      panies pumping oil on their land had headquarters
      in this nearby city.

513. Dickerson, Philip. History of the Osage Nation: Its
      People, Resources and Prospects; The Last Reser-
      vation to Open in the New State. Pawhuska, Okla. :
      Philip Dickerson, 1906. 144 pp.

          Belies its broad title by treating very sketchily
      some of the major events in Osage history.

514.   Dill, Robert Leland.   "Portraits in Red and Black:
       Racial Stereotypes in Oklahoma Newspapers, 1900-
       1925." MA thesis, Texas Christian University,
       1979.

              Contains several references to the Osage mur-
              ders of the 1920s, as well as the opening of the
              reservation in 1906.

515.   Drago, Harry S.   Great American Cattle Trails.   New
       York: Dodd, Mead and Co., 1965.

              Several were in close proximity to the Osages'
              Oklahoma reservation, which cattle drivers used to
              fatten their herds after the long trail from Texas.

516.   Draper, W. R.   "Depression in the Osage," Outlook
       160 (January 27, 1932):   113-114+.

              Tells of the waning royalty money flow from the
              oil fields to the Osages.

517.   Ewing, Charles.   To the President in Regard to the
       Debt Which the Osage Nation Has Petitioned to Pay
       Out of the Proceeds of the Sales of the Osage Lands
       in Kansas.   Washington, D.C.:   n.p., August 31,
       1977.

              This pamphlet concerns the proposal of the Os-
              ages to pay debts accrued by them with Indian trad-
              ers out of tribal funds in the U.S. Treasury.

518.   "Federal Grants Aid Development of Tribal Resources,"
       Osage Nation News (Pawhuska, Oklahoma), Febru-
       ary, 1977.

              Describes the various federally funded programs
              and their administration at the Osage agency at
              Pawhuska, Oklahoma.

519.   Ferber, Edna.   Cimarron.   Garden City, N.Y.: Double-
       day, Doran and Company, Inc., 1930.   388 pp.

A novel based on the author's visits to the Osage country in Oklahoma during the 1920s with
several fictional Osage chracters.

520. Fey, Harold E. , and D'Arcy McNickle. Indians and
Other Americans: Two Ways of Life Meet. New
York: Harper & Brothers, 1959. 220 pp.

One of the earliest histories to be published from
an Indian perspective.

521. Finney, Frank F. "John N. Florer," The Chronicles
of Oklahoma 33 (Summer 1955): 142-144.

A rather laudatory biographical sketch of Florer,
who was the first white trader on the Oklahoma Osage reservation in 1872 and had great influence with
the tribe.

522. Finney, Frank F. "Maria Tallchief in History: Oklahoma's Own Ballerina," The Chronicles of Oklahoma 38 (Fall 1960): 8-11.

Brief sketch of the Osage mixed-blood ballet
dancer who starred in productions in the U. S. and
abroad.

523. Finney, Frank F. "Old Osage Customs Die with the
Last Pah-hue-skah," The Chronicles of Oklahoma
36 (Summer 1958): 131-136.

A short but moving account of the death of the
last Osage chief of the Pah-hue-skah line.

524. Finney, Frank F. "Progress in the Civilization of the
Osage," The Chronicles of Oklahoma 40 (Spring
1962): 2-21.

Based on Finney family records and government
documents, the article covers the early reservation period in Oklahoma.

525.   Finney, Frank F.   "The Indian Territory Illuminating
       Oil Company," The Chronicles of Oklahoma 37 (Sum-
       mer 1959): 149-161.

       The company was a major developer of the Os-
       age oil fields.

526.   Finney, Frank F.   "The Kaw Indians and Their Indian
       Territorial Agency," The Chronicles of Oklahoma
       35 (Winter 1957-1958): 416-424.

       The Kaw, or Kansa, tribe was given a corner
       of the Osage reservation and was administered as
       a subagency until allotment.

527.   Finney, Frank F.   "The Osage Indians and the Liquor
       Problem Before Statehood," The Chronicles of Ok-
       lahoma 34 (Winter 1956): 456-464.

       Alcoholism and alcohol-related social problems
       were a major concern before and after statehood.

528.   Finney, Frank F.   "The Osages and Their Agency Dur-
       ing the Term of Isaac T. Gibson, Quaker Agent,"
       The Chronicles of Oklahoma 36 (Winter 1958-1959):
       416-428.

       Gibson was the first agent (1869-1876) to the
       Osages on their Indian Territory reservation.

529.   Finney, Frank F.   "Trip with the 'Indian Warrior
       Troupe,'" The Chronicles of Oklahoma 32 (Winter
       1954-1955): 381-383.

       In 1879 an agency employee and a missionary
       took a party of Osages through Kansas and Mis-
       souri to perform dances, etc.

530.   Finney, Frank F.   "Troubles of Indian Traders Bring
       Senate Investigation," The Chronicles of Oklahoma
       36 (Spring 1958): 15-20.

In 1885 there was a congressional investigation
of licensed traders, including those on the Osage
reservation.

531. Finney, James Edwin, as told to Joseph B. Thoburn.
      "Reminiscences of a Trader in Osage County," The
      Chronicles of Oklahoma 33 (Summer 1955): 145-158.

      Discusses Finney's experiences as an Indian trader
      with the Pawnee and Osage tribes. Contains de-
      tailed descriptions of Osage hunting, material cul-
      ture, and customs.

532. Finney, Thomas McKean (Wahshowahgaley). Pioneer
      Days with the Osage Indians West of '96. Bartles-
      ville, Okla. : Thomas McKean Finney, 1925. 48
      pp.

      Contains several good photographs and some facts
      not available in more formal histories.

533. Fitzpatrick, W. S. , compiler. Treaties and Laws of
      the Osage Nation as Passed to November 26, 1890.
      Cedar Vale, Kan. : W. S. Fitzpatrick, 1895.

      A useful compilation of legislation passed by the
      constitutional government of the Osages beginning
      in 1881.

534. Forbes, Gerald. "History of the Osage Blanket Leases,"
      The Chronicles of Oklahoma 19 (March 1941): 68-
      77.

      Straightforward account of the disadvantageous
      (to the tribe) block-leasing arrangements of oil com-
      panies drilling for gas and oil on the Osage reser-
      vation.

535. Forbes, Gerald. "Oklahoma Oil and Indian Land Ten-
      ure," Agricultural History 15 (Fall 1941): 189-194.

      Explains the effects of oil on Osage and other
      tribes' land holdings.

536.   Foreman, Carolyn T.   Indians and Pioneers.   New
        Haven: Yale University Press, 1930.

            Has some sketches on the Osages.

537.   Foreman, Carolyn T.   "Journal of a Tour in the In-
        dian Territory," The Chronicles of Oklahoma 10
        (June 1932): 219-256.

            In 1844 N. Sayre Harris of the Protestant Epis-
            copal Church toured several reservations, including
            the Osage.   He provides an interesting description
            of some of their villages.

538.   Foreman, Carolyn T.   Oklahoma Imprints, 1835-1907:
        A History of Printing in Oklahoma Before Statehood.
        Norman: University of Oklahoma Press, 1936.
        499 pp.

            Contains descriptions of Osage Nation newspapers,
            The Osage Magazine, and the Union Mission Press.

539.   Foreman, Grant.   A History of Oklahoma.   Norman:
        University of Oklahoma, 1942.   384 pp.

            The Osages' early history is prominently dis-
            cussed in the first part of the book.

540.   Foreman, Grant.   "J. George Wright, 1860-1941,"
        The Chronicles of Oklahoma 20 (June 1942): 120-
        123.

            Biographical sketch of the Osages' agent during
            their period of oil wealth.

541.   Franks, Kenny A.   The Oklahoma Petroleum Industry.
        Norman: University of Oklahoma Press, 1983.
        300 pp.

            This survey history includes an account of the
            Osage field's development beginning in the 1890s.

542.   Freeman, G. D.   Midnight and Noonday, or Dark Deeds
        Unraveled.   Caldwell, Kan. :   G. D.   Freeman, 1890.

            Within this work the contention is made that Pat-
            rick Hennessey, a freighter on the Chisholm Trail,
            was killed and scalped by Osages in 1874.   How-
            ever, other writers have blamed the Cheyennes for
            the murder.

543.   Gayler, Lucy Boutwell.   "A Case Study in Social Ad-
        justment of One Hundred Osage Families."   MSW
        thesis, University of Oklahoma, 1936.

            Some fairly interesting statistics compiled from
            a study of depression-era tribal families.

543a.   "The Gentle Game of Grab,"   The American Oil Journal
        (April 5, 1917):   4.

            Offers a historical comment on the Foster "blanket
            lease," especially the arrangements involving gas
            wells.

544.   Gibson, Arrell Morgan.   Oklahoma: A History of Five
        Centuries.   Norman, Oklahoma: The Harlow Pub-
        lishing Company, 1965.   523 pp.

            Includes a very good account of the Indian in
            Oklahoma history and is especially useful in under-
            standing Osage affairs before statehood in the con-
            text of Oklahoma and federal Indian policy.

545.   Gibson, Arrell Morgan.   The American Indian: Pre-
        history to the Present.   Lexington, Massachusetts:
        D. C. Heath and Company, 1980.   618 pp.

            Despite its general title, this survey is particu-
            larly strong on Oklahoma Indians, including the Os-
            ages.

546.   Gibson, Arrell M[organ].   The Oklahoma Story.   Nor-

man: University of Oklahoma Press, 1978.   262
pp.

The Osages are included in this popular history
of the state.

547.   Gittinger, Roy.   The Formation of the State of Oklahoma,
       1803-1906.   Norman: University of Oklahoma Press,
       1939.   256 pp.

       Includes a good account of the Osages before
       statehood.

548.   Glasscock, C. B.   Then Came Oil: The Story of the
       Last Frontier.   Indianapolis: The Bobbs-Merrill
       Company, 1938.   349 pp.

       Has a very colorful description of the boom pe-
       riod of Osage oil development in the 1920s.

549.   Grant, Bruce.   American Indians: Yesterday and To-
       day.   New York: E. P. Dutton & Co., Inc., 1958.
       349 pp.

       Has a few references to the Osages, but is not
       a very useful reference since it is not indexed.

550.   Gregory, Robert.   Oil in Oklahoma.   Muskogee, Okla. :
       Leake Industries, 1976.   90 pp.

       Places the development of the rich Osage oil
       and natural gas fields within the context of Okla-
       homa's petroleum industry in its brief overview.

551.   Gridley, Marion E., editor and compiler.   Indians of
       Today.   Chicago: Indian Council Fires Publica-
       tions, Inc., 1971.   494 pp.

       Includes brief biographical sketches of some Os-
       ages, such as Maria and Marjorie Tallchief and
       Yeffe Kimball.

552. Hagan, William T. Indian Police and Judges: Experiments in Acculturation and Control. New Haven: Yale University Press, 1966.

The Osages were among the reservation tribes to inaugurate an agency police force. In their case the effects were mixed, as the author observes.

553. Hager, Jean. "On the Banks of the Arkansas: Blackburn, an Oklahoma Town," The Chronicles of Oklahoma 48 (Winter 1980-1981): 421-431.

Blackburn was founded by an Indian trader on the Osage reservation. The town just across the western border was not appreciated by agents who watched the tribespeople debauched there.

554. Hager, Jean. Yellow-Flower Moon. New York: Doubleday and Company, 1982.

This novel by a Pawnee ranch woman is set in and around Pawhuska and Tulsa with a background of Osage tribal custom. The bond between the Indian protagonist, Maria Hawk, and the land is the book's strongest point.

555. Haines, Joe D. , Jr. "John Stink: The Osage Who 'Returned from the Grave,'" The Chronicles of Oklahoma 60 (Spring 1982): 34-41.

John Stink, Ho-ta-moie, a full-blood Osage, rejected the material comforts offered by the oil royalties accruing to the tribe during the years after World War I and lived aloof and alone in a shanty near the Pawhuska agency golf course until his death in 1938. The legend of his having returned from the grave was the result of newspaper exploitation of an incident when he recovered from hypothermia after apparently being frozen to death.

556. Haines, Joe D. , Jr. "The Log of a Frontier Marshal," The Chronicles of Oklahoma 59 (Fall 1981): 294-303.

A brief sketch of the career of Haines, a deputy
marshal on the Osage reservation for thirty years.
It contains several pages of this peace officer's
log from 1899 and 1900.

557.   Hammons, Terry.   Ranching from the Front Seat of
a Buick: The Life of Oklahoma's A. A. "Jack"
Drummond.   Oklahoma City: Oklahoma Historical
Society, 1982.   258 pp.

Drummond was born on the reservation in 1896
where his father was a trader.   The biography contains some information on the late reservation period and subsequent Osage County ranching.

558.   Hampton, Carol.   "Indian Colonization in the Cherokee
Outlet and Western Indian Territory," The Chronicles of Oklahoma 54 (Spring 1976):   130-145.

Contains information on the move of Osages from
Kansas to Indian Territory.

559.   Hargrett, Lester.   A Bibliography of the Constitutions
and Laws of the American Indians.   Cambridge:
Harvard University Press, 1947.   124 pp.

Among the printed documents relating to the internal government of 14 tribes are those of the Osages.   Included are descriptions of the 1861 and
1881 constitutions.

560.   Haskell Institute Club.   The Osage Nation and History
of Its People.   Pawhuska, Oklahoma: Haskell Institute Club, ca. 1930.   20 pp.

This brief account, a project of Indians who at-
tended the government boarding school at Haskell,
Kansas, contains some interesting details of the
division of the reservation in 1906 and the oil boom
days after World War I.

561.   Hatfield, E. E.   "Economic Survey of Osage County

(1936) Oklahoma with Historical and Geographical Background." Unpublished master's thesis, University of Oklahoma, 1936.

562. Henderson, Felicia. "Informal Report," Dance Magazine 31 (December 1957): 17-18+.

Includes information on Maria and Marjorie Tallchief, sisters who were mixed-blood Osage ballerinas.

563. Hendrix, Kathleen. "Osage Get Out Tribal Vote," The Los Angeles Times, June 1, 1978.

An excellent account with accompanying pictures of the United Osages of Southern California, an organization of tribal headright holders, and the attempts by Oklahoma Osage tribal office seekers to gain their votes.

564. Hertzberg, Hazel W. The Search for an American Indian Identity: Modern Pan-Indian Movements. Syracuse, N. Y.: Syracuse University Press, 1971. 362 pp.

In this study's section on peyote and the Native American Church there are references about the Osages.

565. Hicks, J. C. "Auctions of Osage Oil and Gas Leases." MA thesis, University of Oklahoma, 1949.

Describes the bidding among major and independent oil companies to acquire drilling leases in government run auctions, especially after World War I.

566. Highwater, Jamake. Fodor's Indian America. New York: David McKay Company, Inc., 1975. 431 pp.

A kind of traveler's guide to the residences and reservations of American Indian People. It has some general information on the Osages.

567. Hill, Edward E. Preliminary Inventory of the Records
      of the Bureau of Indian Affairs. 2 vols. Washing-
      ton, D. C. : National Archives and Records Service,
      1965.

568. Hill, Luther B. History of the State of Oklahoma.
      Chicago: n. p. , 1909.

569. Hirschfelder, Arlene B. American Indian and Eskimo
      Authors: A Comprehensive Bibliography. New
      York: Association on American Indian Affairs, 1973.
      99 pp.

570. Holcomb, Gordon Victor. "Some Aspects of Land
      Utilization Among Different Ownership Groups in
      Osage County, Oklahoma. " MS thesis, Oklahoma
      A & M, 1940.

         Mostly interesting for its revelations concerning
      land alienation from the Osages.

571. Howard, James H. "Pan-Indian Culture of Oklahoma,"
      The Scientific Monthly 20 (November 1955): 210-
      215.

         An intriguing analysis of the gradual dimming of
      distinctions among tribal groups in Oklahoma that
      cites the wealthy Osages as the major exception.

572. Huckaby, George Portal. "The Osage Indians and
      Their Treaty Relations with the Federal Govern-
      ment. " MA thesis, Oklahoma A & M, 1936.

         Not much analysis in this rather dry recital of
      treaty terms.

573. Hunt, John Clinton. Generations of Men. Boston:
      Little, Brown and Co. , 1956. 307 pp.

         Set in Oklahoma, this novel deals with the "Che-
      topa Indians" (the author uses a well-known Osage

family name for his fictional tribe) as background
for his white protagonist.

574. Hunt, John Clinton. The Grey Horse Legacy. New
York: Alfred A. Knopf, 1968.   427 pp.

This novel offers a fictional account of the bi-
zarre 1920s "Osage Reign of Terror" in which a
wealthy white cattleman conspired to kill off members of his nephew's wife's family for their shares
in the tribe's oil money.

575. Hunter, Carol. "The Protagonist as a Mixed Blood
in John Joseph Mathews' Novel: Sundown," American Indian Quarterly 6 (Fall/Winter 1982):   319-337.

Mathews was a mixed-blood Osage writer and
novelist whose book Sundown was published in 1934.
Chal Windsor, the mixed-blood main character,
struggles with the turbulence of the Osage oil boom.

576. Hurst, Irwin. The Forty-Sixth Star: A History of
Oklahoma's Constitutional Convention and Early
Statehood.   Oklahoma City: Harlow Publishing Co. ,
1957.

The Osages sent delegates to the convention and
were the subject of special consideration in the
final adopted document.

577. Hynd, Alan. "The Case of the Osage Murders," True:
The Men's Magazine (January 1948): 17-19+.

An incredibly sensationalistic account of the Osage Reign of Terror in the 1920s when several members of the tribe were killed for their oil inheri-
tances.

578. "I Cannot Wait," Newsweek 66 (October 25, 1965):
100.

Profile of Maria Tallchief, an Osage mixed-blood
ballerina.

579. Indian Rights Association. Annual Reports of the Exec-
      utive Committee. 1883-1934.

           These reports contain several articles on the
      Osages written from the notes and observations of
      the association's members visiting the reservations
      in Kansas and Oklahoma.

580. "Indians Retain Strange Rites," The American Indian
      (Tulsa, Oklahoma) 2 (1928): 13.

           Deals briefly with the Osage funeral ceremony
      that included painting the face of the deceased and
      wrapping the body in a blanket before burial.

581. "Indian's Summer," Newsweek 50 (July 15, 1957): 91.

           Deals with Maria Tallchief, a mixed-blood Os-
      age ballerina.

582. Irwin, W. "Richest People on Earth: The Truth About
      Those Osage Indians in Oklahoma," Collier's 76
      (August 22, 1925): 5-6.

           Deals with the tribe's oil wealth and resulting
      exploitation by whites.

583. Jackson, A. P. , and E. C. Cole. Oklahoma. Kansas
      City, Mo. : Ramsey, Millett and Hudson, 1885.

584. Johnson, Steven L. Guide to American Indian Docu-
      ments in the Congressional Serial Set: 1817-1899.
      New York: Clearwater Publishing Co. , 1977. 503
      pp.

585. Jump, Kenneth Jacob. Osage Indian Poems and Short
      Stories. Pawhuska, Okla. : Kenneth Jacob Jump,
      1979. 76 pp.

           Available in local stores and museums in Paw-
      huska, this collection by an Osage newspaper writer

reveals something of the modern manifestations of tribal tradition.

586. Jump, Kenneth Jacob. The Legend of John Stink or Roaring Thunder, "Child of Nature." Pawhuska, Okla. : Kenneth Jacob Jump, 1977. 24 pp.

Privately printed by Osage newspaper writer Jump and drawn from interviews and documents, it relates the life of a full-blood, Ho-tah-moie (John Stink), who rejected the acculturated life of the 1920s and 1930s.

587. Keiser, Albert. The Indian in American Literature. New York: Octagon Books, 1970. 312 pp.

The Osages are discussed in terms of their depiction by Washington Irving and as nouveau riche oil Indians.

588. Keller, Robert H. , Jr. American Protestantism and United States Indian Policy, 1869-82. Lincoln: University of Nebraska Press, 1983. 359 pp.

The Osage tribe's first Quaker agent, Isaac Gibson, and some of his experiences before and after the removal of the tribe from Kansas to Oklahoma are briefly chronicled.

589. Klein, Bernard, and Daniel Icolari, editors. Reference Encyclopedia of the American Indian. New York: B. Klein and Company, 1967. 536 pp.

Arranged topically, there are several references to the Osages.

590. Kohpay, Harry. "Open Doors," Red Man 10 (June 1891): 4.

The author was an Osage who worked as an interpreter at the Osage Agency around the turn of the nineteenth century.

591. Kvasnicka, Robert M., and Herman J. Viola, editors.
      The Commissioners of Indian Affairs, 1824-1977.
      Lincoln: University of Nebraska Press, 1979. 384
      pp.

          Experts in the field of Indian history offer their
          analyses of the Indian Commissioners. Some of
          the articles refer specifically to the Osages.

592. Labadie, George V. A Statement Containing Data in
      Support of the Osage Tribe of Indians' Contention
      that the Present Federal Supervision of Their Af-
      fairs Should Continue to April 8, 1983, and as Long
      as the Minerals Are Produced in Paying Quantities
      with the Osage Indians Paying for Said Supervision.
      Pawhuska, Okla.: Osage Agency, 1954.

          Supports the continuation of the tribal mineral
          estate rather than dividing the reserve's mineral
          resources.

593. La Farge, Oliver, editor. The Changing Indian. Nor-
      man: University of Oklahoma Press, 1942. 184
      pp.

          Perhaps the most relevant aspect of La Farge's
          analysis of Indian America to the Osages is his dis-
          cussion of the unique aspects of Oklahoma Native
          Americans and his discussion of mixed-bloods.

594. Lamb, Arthur H. The Osage People: An Authentic
      Story of the Dim Hazy Past. Pawhuska, Okla.:
      The Osage Printery, ca. 1930. 32 pp.

          A brief commentary on the history of the Osages
          leading up to the end of the reservation era in 1908.

595. Lamb, Arthur H. Tragedies of the Osage Hills. Paw-
      huska, Okla.: Redcorn Press, 1936.

          Most of the stories deal with outlaws attracted
          to the Oklahoma Osage reservation and the social
          ills attending the tribe's wealth.

596. Larson, Charles R. American Indian Fiction. Al-
      buquerque: University of New Mexico Press, 1978.
      208 pp.

      In his analysis of Indian writers Larson includes
      Mathews, the Osage writer, but incorrectly labels
      him an assimilationist.

597. Laws of the Osage Nation Passed at Pawhuska, Osage
      Nation in the Years 1883, 1884, and 1885. Musko-
      gee, Indian Territory: Indian Journal Steam Job
      Office, 1885.

      Has the text of several ordinances passed by the
      constitutional government of the Osage that was in-
      augurated in 1881.

598. Leitch, Barbara. A Concise Dictionary of Indian Tribes
      of North America. Algonac, Mich.: Reference Pub-
      lications, Inc., 1979. 646 pp.

      Arranged by tribe, the entry for the Osages is
      three pages.

599. Levine, Stuart, and Nancy Oestreich Lurie. The Amer-
      ican Indian Today. Baltimore: Penguin Books,
      Inc., 1965. 352 pp.

      Carol Rachlin's chapter on Oklahoma Indians
      deals with that state's Indian population, including
      the Osages during the 1960s. It offers a fairly in-
      formal but informative account of intertribal society
      and pan-Indian activities.

600. Lindquist, G. E. E. The Red Man in the United States:
      An Intimate Study of the Social, Economic and Re-
      ligious Life of the American Indian. New York:
      George H. Doran Company, 1923.

      Obviously influenced by the stories of Osage
      spending during the 1920s oil boom, the author de-
      votes most of his section on the Osages to condemn-
      ing the effects of wealth on the tribe.

601. Logsdon, Guy. "John Joseph Mathews--A Conversa-
      tion," Nimrod 16 (April 1972): 70-75.

          An informative interview of Mathews, the mixed-
      blood Osage writer, which reveals much of his per-
      sonal and professional life with some exceptional
      anecdotes.

602. Marken, Jack W. The American Indian: Language
      and Literature. Arlington Heights, Illinois: AHM
      Publishing Corporation, 1978. 205 pp.

603. Marquis, Arnold. A Guide to America's Indians: Cer-
      emonials, Reservations and Museums. Norman:
      University of Oklahoma Press, 1974. 267 pp.

          The Osages are included in this general survey
      of American Indians in the 1970s.

604. Martin, Viahnett Sprague. Years with the Osages,
      1877-1886. Houston, Texas: Edgemoor Publishing
      Co. , 1889.

          Written by a former Indian Office employee, this
      account of the Osages' Indian Territory reservation
      contains some interesting anecdotes.

605. Mathews, John Joseph. "Admirable Outlaw," The
      Sooner Magazine 2 (April 1930): 241, 264.

          A short story about hunting coyotes on the Os-
      age reservation.

606. Mathews, John Joseph. "Ea Sa Rah N'eah's Story,"
      The Sooner Magazine 3 (June 1931): 328-329.

          A fictional account of an old Osage recounting
      tales of his past as a warrior against the Pawnee.

607. Mathews, John Joseph. "Fred Lookout," The Sunday
      Oklahoman (Oklahoma City, Oklahoma), April 23,
      1939.

Lookout was principal chief of the Osages in the 1930s and 1940s and Mathews' biographical sketch of him draws heavily on oral sources, including the chief.

608. Mathews, John Joseph. "Hunger on the Prairie," The Sooner Magazine 2 (June 1930): 328-329.

A short story about the Osage reservation in winter.

609. Mathews, John Joseph. "Hunting in the Rockies," The Sooner Magazine 1 (May 1929): 263, 278-280.

One of Osage author Mathews' first published pieces.

610. Mathews, John Joseph. Life and Death of an Oilman: The Career of E. W. Marland. Norman: University of Oklahoma Press, 1951.

A sympathetic biography of an oil multimillionaire and governor of Oklahoma, it has a good account of the development of the Osage oil fields.

611. Mathews, John Joseph. "Ole Bob," The Sooner Magazine 5 (April 1933): 206-207.

A short story of the Osage reservation concerning an Indian and his dog.

612. Mathews, John Joseph. "Passing of Red Eagle," The Sooner Magazine 2 (February 1930): 160, 176.

An account of the death rites of a full-blood Osage witnessed by Mathews.

613. Mathews, John Joseph. Sundown. New York: Longmans, Green and Co. , 1934.

A partially autobiographical account, this novel is one of the earliest by an Indian author and deals with the theme of spiritual and economic exploitation of the Osages during the period just prior to World War I through the 1920s.

614.   Mathews, John Joseph. Talking to the Moon. Chicago: University of Chicago Press, 1945. Reissued by the University of Oklahoma Press in 1979, subtitled Wildlife Adventures on the Plains and Prairies of Osage Country, with a foreword by Elizabeth Palmour Mathews. 256 pp.

This was Mathews' favorite work of his own and recounts his experiences living alone in the blackjack forest in Osage County, reflecting on the surroundings and his tribe.

615.   Mathews, John Joseph. The Osages: Children of the Middle Waters. Norman: University of Oklahoma Press, 1961. Paperback edition by University of Oklahoma Press, 1982. 823 pp.

Written by a mixed-blood Osage, it contains a massive ethnohistorical account of the tribe before white contact to 1920. Presented in an almost ahistorical style, it contains invaluable insights gained from the author's personal interviews with tribal elders.

616.   Mathews, John Joseph. Wah'Kon-Tah: The Osage and the White Man's Road. Norman: University of Oklahoma Press, 1932. 359 pp. Paperback edition by University of Oklahoma Press, 1981.

The first university press book ever to be chosen as a Book-of-the-Month Club selection, it was based largely on the diary and correspondence of Quaker agent Laban J. Miles and contains a penetrating analysis of the Osage consciousness.

617.   Maxwell, Amos D. The Sequoyah Constitutional Convention. Boston: Houghton Mifflin Co., 1953.

The Osages sent delegates to participate in the

Oklahoma constitutional convention which ratified the document used for statehood containing special conditions regarding the Osage reservation.

618. Maynard, Olga. Bird of Fire: The Story of Maria Tallchief. New York: Dodd, Mead, 1961. 201 pp.

Primarily concentrates on the career of the Osage mixed-blood ballerina rated among the best in the world.

619. McCoy, Joseph G. Historic Sketches of the Cattle Trade of the West and Southwest. Kansas City, Mo. : Ramsey, Millett and Hudson, 1874.

Some of these included stops at the Osage reservation to fatten cattle before the final push to Kansas railheads.

620. Maclean, Harold Sterns. "Educational Guidance for Osage Indians in the Public Schools." MS thesis, 1939.

621. McReynolds, Edwin C. Oklahoma: A History of the Sooner State. Norman: University of Oklahoma Press, 1954.

The most prominent mention of the Osages is in connection with the 1833 Stokes Commission.

622. McReynolds, Edwin C. ; Alice Marriott; and Estelle Faulconer. Oklahoma: The Story of Its Past and Present. Norman: University of Oklahoma Press, 1967. 485 pp.

The Osages are mentioned frequently and there is a picture of the Pawhuska agency in 1900.

623. Meriam, Lewis, et al. The Problem of Indian Administration. Washington, D. C. : Brookings Institution, 1928.

Among the tribes surveyed were the Osages during the period of oil wealth and resultant exploitation.

624. Meserve, Charles F. A Tour of Observations among Indians and Indian Schools in Arizona, New Mexico, Oklahoma and Kansas. Philadelphia: Indian Rights Association, 1894.

625. Meserve, John Bartlett. " 'Philip Nolan' of the Osages," National Republic 22 (December 1934): 6-7, 28.

Relates with a regrettable, wholly misplaced moralism the legend of the Osage John Stink (Ho-tah-moie) more than the facts of his life.

626. Mills, Lawrence. Oklahoma Indian Land Laws. St. Louis, Mo.: Thomas Law Book Company, 1924. 1,254 pp.

A very useful compendium which has portions of pertinent legislation directly quoted. There is a specific section on the Osage reservation and allotment.

627. Miner, H. Craig. The Corporation and the Indian: Tribal Sovereignty and Industrial Civilization in Indian Territory, 1865-1907. Columbia: University of Missouri Press, 1976.

Devotes a whole chapter to the Osage blanket lease covering oil development beginning in 1896, and also has an excellent analysis of the role of mixed-bloods and full-bloods in tribal politics.

628. Mollin, F. E. "The Cattle Kingdom in Osage County," American Cattle Producer 25 (Fall, 1943): 16-17.

Concentrates on the huge grazing operations that involved leasing the reservation lands before allotment and the buying of large blocks of land from the Osages afterward.

629. "More Athletic, Less Poetic: New York City Ballet
      Company in London," Time 56 (July 24, 1950): 48.

      Maria Tallchief, a mixed-blood Osage, was one
      of the featured ballerinas in the New York company.

630. Morgan, Anne Hodges, editor. Oklahoma Image Ma-
      terials Guide. Norman: Oklahoma Department of
      Libraries, 1981. 190 pp.

      Some works on the Osages are included in this
      annotated bibliography.

631. Morley, Helen Lucile. "A Brief History of the Osage
      Indians." MA thesis, Ohio State University, 1930.

632. Morris, John W. Oklahoma Geography. Oklahoma
      City: Harlow Publishing Co. , 1954.

633. Morris, John W. , and Edwin C. McReynolds. Histori-
      cal Atlas of Oklahoma. Norman: University of
      Oklahoma Press, 1965.

      Contains a map of the Osage reservation with a
      brief historical sketch of the major events in the
      tribe's history after 1871.

634. Morrison, Elting E. , editor. The Letters of Theodore
      Roosevelt. 8 vols. Cambridge: Harvard Univer-
      sity Press, 1952.

      Roosevelt became embroiled in a controversy in-
      volving the Osages and former agent Frank Frantz,
      a Rough Rider who was appointed Oklahoma terri-
      torial governor.

635. Moses, L. G. "Jack Wilson and the Indian Service:
      The Response of the BIA to the Ghost Dance Prophet,"
      American Indian Quarterly 5 (November 1979): 295-
      316.

      Wilson introduced the peyote cult to the Osages.

636. "Most Elaborate Indian Costume in Oklahoma," The
      American Indian (February 1927): 4.

      Has a brief description and a picture of Osage
      Pahsetopah's costume valued at $2,500.

637. Murphy, James E. , and Sharon M. Murphy. Let My
      People Know: American Indian Journalism, 1828-
      1978. Norman: University of Oklahoma Press,
      1981. 230 pp.

      Contains descriptions of The Osage Nation News
      and The Osage Herald.

638. "Native Dancer," Senior Scholastic 68 (April 19, 1956):
      16.

      A profile of the mixed-blood Osage ballerina
      Maria Tallchief.

639. Nett, Betty R. "Historical Changes in the Osage Kin-
      ship System," Southwestern Journal of Anthropology
      8 (1952): 164-181.

      Compiled from field work in Osage County, this
      study emphasizes how the tribe's kinship pattern
      was altered by the economic changes wrought by
      oil money.

640. Nett, Betty R. "Osage Kinship. " MA thesis, Univer-
      sity of Oklahoma, 1951.

      Based on field work done in Osage County, this
      study combines history, ethnohistory, and linguis-
      tics to trace changes in the tribe's kinship patterns.

641. Newman, Tillie Karns. The Black Dog Trail. Boston:
      Christopher Publishing House, 1957. Reissued in
      paperback, 1976. 224 pp.

      A somewhat romantic, informal history of the
      Osages between 1800 and 1900 which contains some

worthwhile quotations and references gleaned from
oral and hard-to-find written and manuscript sources.

642. Nicholson, William. "A Tour of Indian Agencies in
      Kansas and Indian Territory in 1870," The Kansas
      Historical Quarterly 3 (August-November 1934):
      289-326, 343-384.

      The Quaker doctor Nicholson visited the new Os-
      age reservation in Indian Territory on his tour.
      He reports on a speech by Osage mixed-blood Au-
      gust Captaine.

643. Nieberding, Velma. "Catholic Education Among the
      Osage," The Chronicles of Oklahoma 33 (Autumn
      1954): 293-294.

      This well-researched history of Catholic educa-
      tional efforts among the Osages concentrates pri-
      marily on the establishment of the St. Louis and
      St. John's Mission Schools in Indian Territory in
      the 1880s and continues the story to 1917.

644. "Noted Writer, Historian Dies," Osage Nation News
      (Pawhuska, Oklahoma), June 1979.

      Marks the death of the mixed-blood Osage John
      Joseph Mathews and offers a biographical sketch.

645. Nye, Captain W. S. Carbine and Lance: The Story
      of Old Fort Sill. Norman: University of Oklahoma
      Press, 1937. 441 pp.

      Includes a section on the Osages who served as
      scouts for Custer and mentions them in relation to
      several military engagements.

646. O'Beirne, H. F. and E. S. The Indian Territory: Its
      Chiefs, Legislators and Leading Men. St. Louis,
      Missouri: C. B. Woodward Co., 1892.

647.   Olcott, Deana.   The Enchanted Hills.   Pawhuska, Okla-
       homa: The Osage Printery, 1948.

648.   Osage Agency.   The Osage People and Their Trust
       Property: A Field Report of the Bureau of Indian
       Affairs, Anadarko Area Office, Osage Agency, April
       30, 1953.   192 pp.

           An extremely important compilation of material
           concentrating on the Osage mineral estate during
           the period between 1906 and 1952.   It includes sev-
           eral case studies.

649.   Osage Annuity Roll Contested Cases.   Washington, D. C. :
       Government Printing Office, 1898.

           Contains the findings of the Indian Office's inves-
           tigation of the tribal annuity roll members who were
           contested by the tribe as not belonging to the Osage
           Nation and thus not eligible to share in the nation's
           income.

650.   Osage Indian Tribe Centennial Celebration, 1872-1972.
       Tulsa, Oklahoma: Aurora Printing Company, 1972.

           Commemorating the 100th anniversary of the re-
           moval of the tribe from Kansas to Indian Territory,
           this compendium has excellent historical photographs,
           lists of past tribal council memberships, and a brief
           narrative account of Osage history.

651.   Osage Indians Semi-Centennial Celebration, 1907-1957.
       Tulsa, Oklahoma: Aurora Printing Company, 1957.

           Compiled by the Osage agency to commemorate
           the 50th anniversary of Oklahoma statehood cele-
           brated throughout the state in 1957, it contains a
           hodge-podge of information, pictures, and maps on
           the history of the Osages.

651a. The Osage Magazine.   1909-1910.

Printed in Pawhuska, Oklahoma, a broken set
of this rare periodical can be found in the University of Tulsa McFarlin Library's John W. Shleppy
Collection.

652.   "Osage Oil Wealth Fading," Literary Digest 113 (May
       14, 1932): 43.

There was a precipitous drop in royalty payments
to the Osages in the early 1930s following the boom
period of the Twenties.

653.   "Osage Tribal Council," Osage Nation News (Pawhuska,
       Oklahoma), May 1977.

Gives a biographical sketch of each of the members of the tribal council elected in 1976.

654.   "Osage Tribal Glimpses," Literary Digest 89 (April
       3, 1926): 42-44.

A rather lurid exposé type of article describing
the oil boom years of the Osages and the wide variety
of exploiters who came to relieve them of their
"excess" money by legal and illegal means.

655.   "Osage Tribal Original Allottees," Osage Nation News
       (Pawhuska, Oklahoma), June 1978.

This lengthy article of several pages has pictures
and text commemorating and describing the survivors
of the original 2,229 persons listed on the 1906
tribal allotment roll.   Only these persons or their
heirs share in the tribe's mineral estate.

655a. The Osage Troubles in Barbour County, Kansas in the
       Summer of 1874.   Topeka: George W. Martin,
       Kansas Publishing House, 1875.

Contains the correspondence of public officials
in Kansas concerning a skirmish between Osages
and some Kansas citizens in 1874.

656. "Osages Only Tribe with Museum," The Pawhuska
      [Oklahoma] Daily Journal-Capital, April 28, 1938.

      The Museum, which was used for council meet-
      ings as well as housing relics and documents, was
      awarded WPA funds requested in a proposal written
      by John Joseph Mathews.

657. Otis, D. S. The Dawes Act and the Allotment of In-
      dian Lands. Norman: University of Oklahoma
      Press, 1973.

      The Osages and Five Civilized Tribes success-
      fully fought to be excluded from the Dawes Act.

658. Peterson, E. T. "Miracle of Oil," Independent and
      Weekly Review 112 (April 26, 1924): 229.

      Brief comment on the effect of oil on the Osages.

659. Philp, Kenneth R. John Collier's Crusade for Indian
      Reform, 1920-1954. Tucson: University of Ari-
      zona Press, 1977.

      The Osages were kept out of much of Collier's
      plans for an Indian New Deal.

660. "Portrait," Bookman 75 (December 1932): 837.

      A brief background sketch of John Joseph Mathews
      following the publication of Wah'-Kon-Tah and its se-
      lection as a Book-of-the-Month.

661. Pratt, Richard A. Battlefield and Classroom: Four
      Decades with the American Indian, 1867-1904.
      Edited by Robert Utley. New Haven: Yale Uni-
      versity Press, 1964.

      This lengthy personalized account of Indian af-
      fairs by the head of the famous Carlisle Boarding
      School contains some specific references on the Os-
      ages.

662.   Priest, Loring B.   Uncle Sam's Stepchildren: The
       Reformation of United States Indian Policy, 1865-
       1887.   New Brunswick, N.J. :   Rutgers University
       Press, 1942.

       A classic, this study explores the formulation
       and application of the Peace Policy.

663.   Prucha, Francis Paul.   A Bibliographic Guide to the
       History of Indian-White Relations in the United
       States.   Chicago: University of Chicago Press,
       1977.   454 pp.

664.   Prucha, Francis Paul.   Indian-White Relations in the
       United States: A Bibliography of Works Published
       1975-1980.   Lincoln: University of Nebraska Press,
       1982.   179 pp.

665.   Prucha, Francis Paul.   The Churches and the Indian
       Schools, 1882-1912.   Lincoln: University of Ne-
       braska Press, 1979.   278 pp.

       There are many references to the Osages in this
       study of conflict between Catholics and Protestants
       for control of Indian mission schools.

666.   Rahill, Peter J.   The Catholic Indian Missions and
       Grant's Peace Policy, 1870-1884.   Washington,
       D.C. :   Catholic University of America Press, 1953.

       Well-researched, this published dissertation in-
       cludes some fascinating information on the Catholic
       mission to the Osages and its political ramifications.

667.   Records, Ralph H.   "Recollections of the Osages in
       the Seventies," The Chronicles of Oklahoma 22
       (Spring 1944):   70-82.

       Contains some picturesque scenes of early Os-
       age reservation days in Oklahoma during the 1870s
       recalled by a young cook at the agency.

668.   "Regulations for Socio-Economic Fund Released," Os-
       age Nation News (Pawhuska, Oklahoma), August
       1978.

            This lengthy article reprints parts of the federal
            register discussing the implementation of an act of
            October 27, 1972, which provided guidelines for
            the management of Osage judgment funds for edu-
            cation and socioeconomic programs.

669.   Revard, Carter.   "Report to the Nation: Claiming
       Europe," American Indian Quarterly 6 (Fall/Winter
       1982):   305-318.

            Revard, a mixed-blood Osage, offers prose and
            poetry about an Indian's perspective of modern Eu-
            rope.

670.   "Richest Indians," Literary Digest 122 (December 12,
       1936):   14.

            A brief comment on those Osages, mostly full-
            bloods, who had accumulated large bank accounts
            and retained them after the oil boom of the 1920s.

671.   "Richest People Per Capita on Earth Get $8,290,100
       for Oil Leases," Current Opinion 74 (June 1923):
       740-741.

            A brief account of competitive bidding by oil
            companies to obtain leases on tracts of the Osage
            mineral estate.

672.   Rogers, S.   "Red Men in Gas Buggies: The Tale of
       an Auction with Million-Dollar Bids," Outlook 134
       (August 22, 1923):   629-632.

            Describes the competitive bidding among oil com-
            panies paying up to a million dollars and more for
            the drilling lease rights on 160-acre tracts of the
            Osages' mineral estate.

673.   Rohrer, J. H. "The Test Intelligence of Osage In-
        dians," Journal of Social Psychology 16 (Spring
        1959): 99-105.

674.   Ross, Norman A. , editor. Index to the Decisions of
        the Indian Claims Commission. New York: Clear-
        water Publishing Co. , 1973.

675.   Ross, Norman A. , editor. Index to the Expert Testi-
        mony Before the Indian Claims Commission. New
        York: Clearwater Publishing Co. , 1974. 102 pp.

676.   Russell, Orpha B. "Chief James Bigheart of the Os-
        ages," The Chronicles of Oklahoma 32 (Winter 1954-
        1955): 384-394.

        Bigheart was a leading figure in tribal politics
        during the first decades of the Indian Territory
        reservation days and was the main mover in the
        formation of the 1881 constitutional government.
        This article has some information from oral sour-
        ces not available elsewhere.

677.   Schmeckebier, Laurence F. The Office of Indian Af-
        fairs: Its History, Activities and Organization.
        Baltimore: The Johns Hopkins Press, 1927. 591
        pp.

        The author offers a brief history of the Osage
        tribe's relations with the U. S. with a lengthy quo-
        tation from an Indian inspector on the effect of oil
        wealth on the people.

678.   Scott, John. "The County Osage," Oklahoma Monthly
        4 (April 1978): 41-53, 74-86.

        A well-written journalistic impression of the
        Osages and their neighbors during the renewed
        boom in oil development of the late 1970s stemming
        from the Arab embargo.

679. Seely, O. C. Oklahoma Illustrated: A Book of Prac-
     tical Information. Guthrie, Oklahoma Territory,
     Leader Printing, 1894.

680. Seymour, Flora Warren. The Story of the Red Man.
     New York: Longmans, Green and Company, 1929.
     421 pp.

681. Shepherd, W. G. "Lo, The Rich Indian," Harper's
     Monthly Magazine 141 (November 1920): 723-734.
     Condensation in Literary Digest 67 (November 20,
     1920): 62-64.

     A popular commentary on the effects of oil wealth
     on the Osages.

682. Shirley, Glenn. West of Hell's Fringe: Crime, Crim-
     inals, and the Federal Peace Officer in Oklahoma
     Territory, 1889-1907. Norman: University of Ok-
     lahoma Press, 1978. 495 pp.

     The Osage reservation was the scene of much
     crime and appears often in the narrative that is
     very well written and researched.

683. Slosson, E. E. "Lo! The Rich Indian," Independent
     and Weekly Review 103 (September 18, 1920): 337-
     338.

     Another sensationalistic account of the Osages
     and their oil wealth.

684. Spicer, Edward H. A Short History of the Indians of
     the United States. New York: D. Van Nostrand
     Company, 1969. 319 pp.

     This general history includes a description of
     the unique status of the modern Osages.

685. Stewart, Dora Ann. The Government and Development
     of Oklahoma Territory. Oklahoma City: Harlow
     Publishing Company, 1933. 434 pp.

Has many extended references to the Osages and
the tribe's reservation in the politics that led to
statehood.

686.   Strickland, Rennard. The Indians in Oklahoma. Norman: University of Oklahoma Press, 1980. 171
pp.

This well-written narrative has many references
to the Osages and pictures of tribal members. The
volume contains excellent maps, statistical tables,
etc. , but no index.

687.   Sutton, Imre. Indian Land Tenure: Bibliographical
Essays and a Guide to the Literature. New York:
Clearwater Publishing Company, 1975. 290 pp.

Includes a discussion of the works of three writers
who have dealt with Osage land.

688.   Sweet, Evander M. "Richest People in the World,"
World To-Day 5 (November 1903): 1454-1458.

This article, appearing fifteen years before the
Osage oil money grew to noticeable proportions,
shows that the tribe enjoyed a considerable income
from grazing leases, timber cutting, and other sources.

689.   "Talented Tallchief: We Find Our Own Ballerina,"
Newsweek 44 (October 11, 1954): 102+.

Profile of Maria Tallchief, the mixed-blood Osage ballerina.

690.   Taylor, R. C. "The Geology of the Foraker Area, Osage County, Oklahoma. " Unpublished master's thesis, University of Oklahoma, 1953.

691.   Taylor, Theodore W.   The States and Their Indian
Citizens. Washington, D.C. , 1972. 307 pp.

The parts of this study dealing with termination
policy and the incorporation of tribes contain information on the Osages.

692.   "Terpsichorean Tallchief," Theatre Arts 42 (September
        1958): 66.

        Deals with Maria Tallchief, the mixed-blood Os-
        age ballerina.

693-   Terry, W. "Maria Tallchief and the Maryinsky Tradi-
96.   tion," Theatre Arts 45 (September 1961): 57-59+.

        Tallchief was a mixed-blood Osage ballerina.

697.   Thoburn, Joseph B. A Standard History of Oklahoma.
        New York: The American Historical Society, 1916.

698.   Thomas, Clarence Lot, editor. Annotated Acts of Con-
        gress: Five Civilized Tribes and the Osage Nation.
        Columbia, Mo. : E. W. Stephens Publishing Com-
        pany, 1913. 347 pp.

        A very useful compendium that includes many of
        the acts of Congress pertaining to and uniquely af-
        fecting the Osages.

699.   Thomas, Sister M. Ursala. "The Catholic Church on
        the Oklahoma Frontier, 1824-1907." Ph. D. dis-
        sertation, St. Louis University, 1938.

        Includes much information on the Catholic work
        with the Osages before statehood, especially the
        organization and administration of the reservation
        boarding schools.

700.   Tinker, Sylvester. "What IECW Means to the Osage,"
        Indians at Work 3 (September 15, 1935): 11-16.

        Tinker, a mixed-blood Osage, wrote positively
        about the effect of the 1930s Indian division of the
        Civilian Conservation Corps.

701. Truve, A. W. von. "Two WPA Projects of Historical
      Interest," Southwestern Historical Quarterly 42 (Win-
      ter 1938): 117-121.

      One of the two projects described is the Osage
      Tribal Museum, the nation's first Indian-owned mu-
      seum, which was built in Pawhuska, Oklahoma with
      funds generated by a grant written by mixed-blood
      councilman John Joseph Mathews.

702. Tyler, S. Lyman. A History of Indian Policy. Wash-
      ington, D. C. : United States Department of the In-
      terior, Bureau of Indian Affairs, 1973. 328 pp.

703. U. S. Department of Commerce. Federal and State In-
      dian Reservations and Indian Trust Areas. Washing-
      ton, D. C. : Government Printing Office, 1973. 604
      pp.

      Offers a brief and not always accurate survey
      of the Osages' history, culture, and land status.

704. Vanderwerth, W. C. Indian Oratory: Famous Speeches
      by Noted Indian Chieftains. Norman: University
      of Oklahoma Press, 1971. 292 pp.

      Includes a brief speech by Osage chief Joseph
      Paw-ne-no-pashe (Big Hill or Governor Joe).

705. Vehik, Susan C. "The Osage Allotment: A Prelimin-
      ary Analysis of Land Selection Patterns," in John
      H. Moore, editor, Special Volume, "Ethnology in
      Oklahoma," Papers in Anthropology 21 (Fall 1980):
      93-105.

      Using statistical analysis, the author attempts
      to show that half-blood Osages tended to choose
      arable land in selecting homestead allotments when
      the reservation was divided in 1906, whereas the
      full-bloods tended to choose according to kinship
      and other traditional ties.

706.   Velie, Alan R., editor. <u>American Indian Literature,</u>
       <u>An Anthology.</u> Norman: University of Oklahoma
       Press, 1979.

            Included are excerpts from the writings of Os-
            age mixed-bloods, John Joseph Mathews and Carter
            Revard.

707.   Wax, Murray L., and Robert W. Buchanan, editors.
       <u>Solving "The Indian Problem":</u> The White Man's
       <u>Burdensome Business.</u> New York: The New York
       Times Company, 1975. 237 pp.

            Some of the essays included in this volume touch
            on Osage tribal government and peyote use.

708.   Weathers, Winston. <u>Indian and White: Sixteen Eclogues.</u>
       Lincoln: University of Nebraska Press, 1970. 105
       pp.

            A third of these impressionistic writings and
            poems deal with the Osages on the subjects of John
            Stink, Pah-se-to-pah, the August dances, the rite
            of the chiefs, and the tribal religion.

709.   Westbrook, Harriet Johnson. "And 'Twas the Night
       Before Christmas' with Osages; by O-Jan-Jan-Win,"
       <u>The American Indian</u> (Tulsa, Oklahoma) 4 (1929):
       8.

710.   White, Eugene E. <u>Experiences of a Special Indian</u>
       <u>Agent.</u> Norman: University of Oklahoma Press,
       1965.

            Includes some good descriptive passages of the
            early Indian Territory agency days.

711.   White, Lonnie. "Indian Soldiers of the 36th Division,"
       <u>Military History of Texas and the Southwest</u> 15 (1979):
       7-20.

            The Osages were among the Oklahoma Indians that
            served in the 36th Division during World War I.

712. Whitehead, Donald F.   The FBI Story: A Report to
      the People.   New York: Random House, 1956,
      368 pp.

          Includes a narrative account of the 1920s Osage
      murders, a series of crimes investigated by the
      FBI.

713. Whitham, Louise Morse.   "Herbert Hoover and the
      Osages," The Chronicles of Oklahoma 25 (Spring
      1947):   2-4.

          Hoover spent a year at the Osage agency in Paw-
      huska, Oklahoma with Agent Laban Miles in 1882.

714. Wilson, Raymond.   "Dr. Charles A. Eastman's Report
      on the Economic Conditions of the Osage Indians in
      Oklahoma, 1924," 60 (Fall 1977):   343-345.

          The report is simply a letter, but it does offer
      a trained observer's impression, mostly negative,
      of the tribe's sudden oil wealth.

714a. Wilson, Terry P.   "Chief Fred Lookout and the Politics
      of Osage Oil, 1906-1949," Journal of the West 23
      (July 1984):   46-53.

          Biographical essay on Fred Lookout, elected
      principal chief of the Osages numerous times be-
      ginning in 1913.

715. Wilson, Terry P.   "Osage Indian Women During a Cen-
      tury of Change, 1870-1980," Prologue: Journal of
      the National Archives 14 (Winter 1982):   185-201.

          Concentrates on the ways in which female Os-
      ages dealt with the forces of acculturation and those
      white men who preyed on them for their wealth.

716. Wilson, Terry P.   "Osage Oxonian: The Heritage of
      John Joseph Mathews," The Chronicles of Oklahoma
      59 (Fall 1981):   264-293.

Offers a biographical sketch and critical analysis of the career and writings of the mixed-blood Osage who was a council member in the 1930s and wrote five books about his tribe and county.

717. Wilson, Terry P. Underground Reservation: Osage Oil. Lincoln: University of Nebraska Press, forthcoming 1985.

Based on archival and oral sources, this study concentrates on the effects of oil wealth on the Osages and the progress of internal tribal politics and culture between 1871 and 1981.

718. Wilson, Terry P. "Women of the Osage: A Century of Change, 1874-1982," in Melvena K. Thurman, editor, Women in Oklahoma: A Century of Change. Oklahoma City: Oklahoma Historical Society, n.d., pp. 57-102.

A lengthier version of a similar piece that appeared in Prologue: Journal of the National Archives, it contains ethnographic and historical information on female Osages during the reservation period and after.

719. Woolery, John. "Major General Clarence L. Tinker," The Chronicles of Oklahoma 27 (Autumn 1949): 238-242.

Offers a short biographical sketch of Tinker, a mixed-blood Osage who achieved the rank of general in the Army Air Corps during World War II.

720. Wright, J. George. Index to the Certified Roll of Members of the Osage Tribe of Indians in Oklahoma. Washington, D.C.: U.S. Department of the Interior, 1921.

The 1908 annuity roll was divided into two parts in 1921: Osages of less than one-half Indian blood and those of more. The index indicates original roll numbers, allotment numbers, degrees of Indian

blood, and dates of birth. Copies are available
from the Osage Tribal Museum in Pawhuska, Oklahoma.

721. Wright, Muriel H. A Guide to the Indian Tribes of
      Oklahoma. Norman: University of Oklahoma Press,
      1951.

      Has a good brief summation of the Osages, their
      history and culture.

722. Wright, Peter M. "John Collier and the Oklahoma In-
      dian Welfare Act of 1936," The Chronicles of Okla-
      homa 60 (Autumn 1972): 347-371.

      An excellent analysis of the politics surrounding
      the rejection by Oklahoma tribes of the Wheeler
      Howard Act and subsequent adoption of the 1936
      legislation from which only the Osages were ex-
      cluded.

AUTHOR INDEX